Robert Kent
1 1 2 N 45 Apt 12
Nyc 36
~~Columbus 5 6 9 9~~
Judson-6-7129

BY
ANDRÉ GIDE

Non-Fiction

THE JOURNALS OF ANDRÉ GIDE
Volume I, 1889–1913   Volume II, 1914–1927
Volume III, 1928–1939   Volume IV, 1939–1949

IMAGINARY INTERVIEWS

THE FRUITS OF THE EARTH
(*Les Nourritures terrestres* & *Les Nouvelles Nourritures*)

Fiction and Theater

THE COUNTERFEITERS
(with *Journal of "The Counterfeiters"*)

THE IMMORALIST

LAFCADIO'S ADVENTURES

STRAIT IS THE GATE

TWO SYMPHONIES
(*Isabelle* & *The Pastoral Symphony*)

THE SCHOOL FOR WIVES, ROBERT, and GENEVIÈVE

TWO LEGENDS
(*Œdipus* & *Theseus*)

MY THEATER
(*Saul, Bathsheba, Philoctetes, King Candaules,
Persephone,* & the essay "The Evolution of the Theater")

THESE ARE BORZOI BOOKS
PUBLISHED BY ALFRED A. KNOPF IN NEW YORK

ANDRÉ GIDE

My Theater

Alfred A. Knopf

NEW YORK

1952

ANDRÉ GIDE

My Theater

FIVE PLAYS AND AN ESSAY

SAUL

BATHSHEBA

PHILOCTETES

KING CANDAULES

PERSEPHONE

The Evolution of the Theater

TRANSLATED FROM THE FRENCH BY

Jackson Mathews

L. C. catalogue card number: 51–11098

THIS IS A BORZOI BOOK,
PUBLISHED BY ALFRED A. KNOPF, INC.

FIRST AMERICAN EDITION

Contents

Saul

A PLAY IN FIVE ACTS

1896

TO EDOUARD DE MAX

CHARACTERS

SAUL

DAVID

JONATHAN

THE QUEEN

SAKI, *a cupbearer*

NABAL, *the High Priest*

JONAS, *a barber*

ELIPHAS

JOEL, *a servant*

THE WITCH OF ENDOR

THE GHOST OF SAMUEL

AN OLD JEW

A CHILD

Demons, servants, guards,
messengers, soldiers, Jews

ACT I

THE KING'S PALACE: *A vast barren hall; on the right, doors leading to the inner part of the palace; on the left, window recesses over which curtains are drawn. In the back, a wide opening; to right and left, massive columns replace the wall; in the middle, the space between the columns is filled by an enormous throne. Between the columns the view extends onto a terrace, and out over the gardens, where the tops of trees are seen. It is night. At the end of the terrace, KING SAUL may be seen, in moonlight, praying. Near by, HIS CUPBEARER, asleep.*

SCENE I

DEMONS *enter through the window recesses, stirring and lifting the curtains. Others from other directions.*

DEMONS: Could you tell us the way to the palace, please?

FIRST DEMON: This is it.

DEMONS: Ha ha! That's a good one! We were together awhile ago, and here you are to welcome us! How did you get in?

3

FIRST DEMON: Sh! Sh! Not so loud, there's the King.
[*He points.*]

THIRD DEMON: Where? [*Sees him.*] Aha! Who is that
with him?

FIRST DEMON: A cupbearer.

SECOND DEMON: What is the King doing?

THIRD DEMON: Sleeping?

FIRST DEMON: No, praying. Speak softly.

THIRD DEMON: I'm speaking softly enough; if I disturb
him, it's because he isn't praying hard enough.

FOURTH DEMON: He's doing the best he can.

FIRST DEMON: Where are the others?

SECOND DEMON: They are coming.

FIRST DEMON: Hurry! Come in! Come in! Is everybody
here?

[*Enter more* DEMONS.]

SECOND DEMON: There's no way to tell. Some are still
hanging back in the desert.

FIRST DEMON: And now tell me: is it true that he has
had all our masters murdered?

SEVERAL DEMONS: Yes; all of them.

FIFTH DEMON: No, not all. He spared the witch of
Endor.

SECOND DEMON: Oh! She never had any real demons at
her place; just a few grunting toads.

FIRST DEMON: But tell me about the sorcerers.

FIFTH DEMON: All killed—to the last one!

FIRST DEMON: Too bad for King Saul! Since he's the one

4

who has had us thrown out of our lodging, we'll come and lodge with him.

FOURTH DEMON: But why did he have the sorcerers killed?

SECOND DEMON: Stupid! To be the only one to know the future.

FOURTH DEMON: The only one who tries to know it, you mean.

THIRD DEMON: If you try long enough, it's here.

SIXTH DEMON: What is the most unknown of all futures?

FIFTH DEMON: One that never comes. [*All laugh.*]

FIRST DEMON: Lot of dim-wits! Try to be serious. First let's look to our lodging; you can laugh later. Let's divide the work fairly, each according to his talents. Now one at a time, tell me what suits you [*they stir*] —but wait till I ask. You, over there, say: what do you choose? Give me a good answer.

SIXTH DEMON: His cup. I am anger, madness: when he seeks comfort in drink, he will find me.

FIRST DEMON: Good. Now you?

FIFTH DEMON: For me, his bed—I'm lust. I'll be there when he tries to sleep.

FIRST DEMON [*to another*]: And what are you?

FOURTH DEMON: Fear—I'll sit on this throne, and when I blow upon him, his hopes will tremble like a candle flame. I am also doubt. When I whisper, he will take it for advice.

FIRST DEMON: And you?

5

THIRD DEMON: I choose his scepter. It will be heavy in
his hands and heavy on others' shoulders when he
strikes; but slight and trembling as a reed when he
wants to prop his weakness on it. My name will be
rule.

ANOTHER DEMON [*at* FIRST DEMON's *nod*]:   I choose his
purple, my name is vanity. He will be naked under
his purple robes; and when the wind blows he will
shiver in his purple; and when it is hot, my name will
be indecency.

FIRST DEMON: I take his crown. My name is Legion. And
now, my friends, we can laugh. Say there, pass me my
crown! Lift my purple train! And someone hold my
spear and carry this cup before me, so you may see
how a king chases after it—chases after it with all his
glory! [*Puts on the King's robes left lying on the
throne; the demons form a grotesque cortège.*] The
King is stirring! Look out! Day is breaking! Quick! To
your posts! We must be gone! [*They put the King's
robes back in their place on the throne and disappear,
as it were, inside the throne.* KING SAUL *comes slowly
forward.*]

SCENE II

[SAUL]

SAUL: I am still King Saul—but there is a point past
which I can no longer know. There was a time when

6

God would answer me; but in those times, it's true, I
asked Him very little. Every morning the priest would
tell me what I was to do: that was the whole future;
and I knew the future. It was I who made it. Then the
Philistines came; I was uneasy; I tried to find answers
in myself; and from that moment God fell silent. But
how did He expect me to act? In order to act rightly,
I have to know the future. For a time, I discovered
something in the stars; for twenty nights I have looked,
patiently. I saw nothing having to do with the Philistines. But that's a small matter now. What I did discover has made me an old man: Jonathan, my son
Jonathan, is not the one who will succeed me on the
throne, and my line will end. But who will take my
place, that I cannot find out—and for twenty nights
I have been trying; tonight I even tried praying again.
The nights are too short in summer; it is so hot that
nothing, no one around me, can sleep; no one but my
tired cupbearer; I need others to sleep; I am constantly
being distracted. The slightest noise, the slightest
fragrance, takes my attention; my senses are turned
outward and no sweetness passes me unperceived.

Last night my servants went out, on my orders, and
killed the sorcerers—ah, the last sorcerer in Israel!
None but myself must know my secret. And when I
am the only one who knows the future, I believe I
will be able to change it. They are dead now; I know
they are dead: about midnight I felt my secret suddenly expand; when I alone held it, it occupied a

7

larger place in my heart—and oppressed me. It is all mine!

Look, day is here! Let everyone in the palace be awakened! I shall sleep for a while. Last night I composed some songs that I must show to the high priest; I want him to sing them and have them sung all over the kingdom. [*He puts on his robes, sets the crown on his head, takes up the scepter, and exits, saying:*] Yes! I am Saul still. And I have servants in great number.

SCENE III

Two SERVANTS *enter with brooms on their shoulders.*

FIRST SERVANT: Say! Did you see him?

SECOND SERVANT (JOEL):   Who?

FIRST SERVANT: The King.

SECOND SERVANT: The King?

FIRST SERVANT: Sure! We've found him here for the last three nights. When we come on the terrace, he runs. I don't know what he can be up to, but, skinny as he is, it's surely not prayers.

[*They sweep, then raise one of the vast curtains on the left. Daylight comes in.*]

JOEL [*seeing the* CUPBEARER *asleep*]:   Look, it's Saki! Hey, cupbearer! That's no place to sleep. Come on, up! What are you doing here, my boy?

8

SAKI [*waking*]: The King—

FIRST SERVANT [*pretending to sweep him off*]: The King! That's me; the king of sweepers! [SAKI *gets up*.] But say! Let's talk about the King. A fine spree he goes on, out here on the terrace! Huh?

JOEL: Shut up, fool! . . . Tell me, my boy, did the King spend the night out here?

SAKI: Yes.

JOEL: The whole night?

SAKI: Yes.

JOEL: All night—every night?

SAKI: For the last ten days or more.

JOEL: And what do you do?

SAKI: I pour his drinks.

FIRST SERVANT: And what does he do?

SAKI: He drinks.

FIRST SERVANT: That's disgusting, a king getting drunk.

SAKI: Saul doesn't get drunk.

FIRST SERVANT [*sneering*]: It's because you don't pour him enough.

JOEL: Shut up, fool! What were you saying, my boy; tell me. What does the King do out here all night?

SAKI: He says he would like to be drunk, but can't; he says wine isn't strong enough. Sometimes he looks at the sky and talks as if he were alone.

JOEL: What does he say?

SAKI: I don't know; but he looks very troubled. Sometimes he falls to his knees as if he is going to pray, but then he doesn't say anything at all. Yesterday he asked

me if I knew how to pray; I said yes, and then he told
me to pray for the prophets; I thought he was joking,
and I said the prophets were supposed to pray for us;
then he said you have to pray before you get to be a
prophet, because afterwards you can't—and a lot of
other things I didn't understand very well, but they
made him laugh and cry.

JOEL: And what else?

SAKI: He tells me I must be tired and that I must sleep.

JOEL: And do you sleep?

SAKI: Yes, I go to sleep.

[*Pause.*]

JOEL: You love the King, my boy?

SAKI: Yes, I love the King; very much.

JOEL: Too bad.

SAKI: Why do you say too bad?

JOEL: No matter, too bad!

SAKI: Of course I love the King; he is good to me; he
makes me take sips from his cup and then smiles so
gently when the wine is too strong for me. He talks to
me; he says he is happy only at night, but even at
night daytime worries torment him. He says he was
happy when he was young, and that he has not always been King.

FIRST SERVANT: That's so, all right!

SAKI: Is it true that he has not always been King?

FIRST SERVANT: He was a herdsman, like us.

SAKI: So it's true, what he told me, that one time he
went a long way into the desert, for twenty days and

10

twenty nights, looking for some stray asses; I thought he was joking too when he said that the happiest moment he ever had was when he was searching for those asses in the desert. But he never found them. He said too that when he was young he was very handsome—the fairest of the children of Israel, so he said. He's still very handsome, isn't he, King Saul?

FIRST SERVANT:　King Saul is a little jaded. If he keeps on this way every night, sticking his nose into the stars—

JOEL:　Shut up, fool! Go to bed, my boy; after a night like that, morning is not good for anything but sleep. [*Aside*] Nothing doing with that boy.

[SAKI *starts to go; the first servant snatches the jug from his hands.*]

FIRST SERVANT:　Hey, just leave that with us! You don't want to sleep with a jug! [SAKI *waits.*] Go on! Good-by, good-by!

SCENE IV

[THE TWO SERVANTS]

FIRST SERVANT [*drinks*]:　He's crazy.

JOEL:　Who?

FIRST SERVANT:　The King. He's crazy! [*Drinks.*] He's mad! He's mad! It's all right with me if a man wants to stay up all night drinking wine like this; or even praying if he has something on his stomach he can't digest;

11

or even looking at the sky to see what tomorrow's
weather will be. But all three at once! [*Drinks.*] I tell
you, he's crazy! [*Drinks.*]

JOEL [*preoccupied*]:   Shut up, fool! [*Aside*] He's too
young and simple-minded; we won't learn anything
from him.

FIRST SERVANT: Ah, hah! The high priest! When the
King goes to bed, he gets up.

SCENE V

———————————

[THE TWO SERVANTS, THE HIGH PRIEST,
THEN THE QUEEN]

HIGH PRIEST [*to the* FIRST SERVANT]:   Go elsewhere to do
your sweeping. [*Exit* FIRST SERVANT.]

Tell me, Joel! Have you seen the King? Did he talk
about himself? What did you learn? Tell me, what
did you learn? I have come early because I need to
know how matters stand, before he has seen the messengers, so as to meet any new resolves he may take.
The messengers are already back; their abominable
work is done; and the clamors of the people have
wakened the King, if indeed he was still asleep.

JOEL: Not still, but already. For a long time now the
King has been keeping watch every night on the terrace.

HIGH PRIEST: Under the stars. Well, well! . . . Alone?

JOEL: Yes. . . . No: with the cupbearer.

HIGH PRIEST: The boy. . . . Will he talk? Come, tell me; what did you find out?

JOEL: Your questions come too fast; and anyway, I didn't find out anything.

HIGH PRIEST: What does the boy say?

JOEL: Nothing that matters.

HIGH PRIEST: He's too young. Does the King drink too much?

JOEL: He says he can't get drunk.

HIGH PRIEST: Then we shall have to find something else.

JOEL: The Queen!

[*Enter the* QUEEN.]

HIGH PRIEST [*to her*]:   Nothing yet, Madam, still nothing.

[*Silence.*]

QUEEN [*to the* SERVANT]:   Does he talk to the cupbearer?

JOEL: No; to himself. . . .

QUEEN: And—he says?

JOEL: The boy can't recall a thing.

HIGH PRIEST: That is what I feared, Madam; he is too young.

QUEEN: We shall have to find someone else.

HIGH PRIEST [*stopping the* SERVANT, *who is about to go*]:   Joel! . . . Once more. What does Saki say about the King?

JOEL: He says he loves him.

13

HIGH PRIEST [*to the* QUEEN]: And, you see: he has won the boy's affection.

[*Exit* JOEL.]

SCENE VI

[THE HIGH PRIEST, THE QUEEN]

HIGH PRIEST: There is no longer any doubt, Madam: the King has a secret. He is seeking to read the stars. And I think he has had the sorcerers killed because, once he has read the stars, he wants to be the only one who knows what they say. . . . The Queen knows, no doubt, that Saul is now spending his nights on the terrace?

QUEEN: Ah, Nabal, how could I know? [*The* HIGH PRIEST *smiles.*] Oh! it was so long ago that Saul withdrew from me. . . . Nabal! Today my anxiety is so great that I must speak to you more fully. Nabal! Saul has never loved me. He pretended, when he married me, to feel some passion for me; but it was a compulsion that could not last—and you have no idea, Nabal, how cold his embraces were! As soon as I was with child, they ceased. For a while I feared that I might have cause to be jealous, but it was a mistaken fear: there was nothing. I know, I know he had concubines; but now he has put them all away—and shall I tell you this, Nabal? Jonathan, Jonathan is the only child that is his. He dropped from my bosom before his time, like a green fruit to wither before it ripens. It was a long time before the shame of such a sickly offspring was quiet in me. I weaned him early, for I wished this weakling to be under the sole influence of men, thinking for a long time that to live among warriors would perhaps exalt his courage. He hardly knows me at all. I am the Queen, not his mother. He fears me, not loves me. It took some time, I confess, to stifle every impulse in my heart and give myself, as I do today, wholly to the difficult questions of the kingdom. Saul is happy to help me in nothing; his negligence is incredible; and yet he is always preoccupied. Nabal! Nabal! How I suffered, at first, to see Saul's anxiety stamped on the brow of his feeble son. Sometimes I used to follow the boy as he wandered in the gardens or in the shadowy corridors of the palace; never have I seen him smile. And my hatred turned upon Saul for having created, through me, a piteous posterity in his own hideous image.

HIGH PRIEST: Yet Saul used to be very handsome.

QUEEN: Jonathan too is very handsome. . . . I know. I know, his weak body has a kind of grace; but I hate his weakness, Nabal; I hate him; I hate him! I hate him!

But I did not call you away from your prayers to speak of him. Listen, it is not that the King's anxiety bothers me; I like to know that he is occupied. The anxieties of love are harder, more wearing than those of the

kingdom; the latter distract me from the former. Besides, I like to feel my power; and the King made no
demands at all. Everything was going well: the God
of Israel too was extending His power and prospering
from my rule. And now, Nabal—

HIGH PRIEST: And now—!

QUEEN: We had him so well in hand, Nabal.

HIGH PRIEST: Yes, but for the past month he has completely escaped us.

QUEEN: It seems that I can do nothing so long as I do
not know what he is thinking. The Philistines are there,
waiting. Saul alone can give an order; but it was I who
ruled his will. Through him I held full power. At least
he listened to what I told him, through your lips. But
now, as you say, he has escaped us; and while the
Philistines stand at the gates, neither attacking nor
retiring, while they mock the inertia of our men, Saul
watches them from the terraces and seems to be thinking of something else.

HIGH PRIEST: The Philistines mock us, it is true; they
have even found new means of making fun of us: a
hideous man named Goliath, taller by a head than the
tallest. For the last four days, every morning we have
heard a trumpet blast; then a little soldier walks out
ahead of the big one, and up and down they parade
in front of our army. Goliath calls out his challenge
to anyone to meet him in combat; he proposes to decide
the battle by this peculiar kind of match. Our army
looks at him in silence, and no one volunteers; so every

16

morning the giant's arrogance is greater, his defiance more mocking, his insults more outrageous. Soon he will consider himself already victorious; he will have won without a fight, a victory by mutual agreement! Our soldiers no longer even take themselves seriously; this war is just a game they joke about. Trading is carried on between the two armies; as soon as the morning challenge is over, the men break camp bounds, mix and mingle with one another, exchange tools, gods, love, and merchandise; Saul keeps his silence, and Israel, once tough, is little by little softening.

QUEEN: What did you say this giant's name is?

HIGH PRIEST: Goliath!

QUEEN: Do you know of no one to put against him?

HIGH PRIEST: No one yet.

QUEEN: And no one to replace the cupbearer?

HIGH PRIEST: The barber is seeing to that. But why replace him? The King would suspect something; he is attached to the boy. It would be better to create a new post: a singer, a guitar-player, or something of that sort.

QUEEN: But who is going to persuade the King to accept him? He distrusts us and he will no longer allow a stranger in his presence. . . . Jonas the barber must work on him; he knows how to handle Saul; he leads him on and the King lets him talk.

HIGH PRIEST: Is he coming?

QUEEN: Coming with Saul directly.

HIGH PRIEST: Here they are, both.

17

SCENE VII

[THE SAME, WITH SAUL AND THE BARBER
JONAS, AND GUARDS; THEN JONATHAN; THEN
MESSENGERS]

QUEEN [*eagerly*]:   Saul, my lord, how did you pass the
night? You are quite pale; as if the moonlight were still
on your forehead. Believe me, it is a mistake for you
to stay out so long on the terrace. [SAUL *gestures.*]
They say the full moons of summer are injurious to our
thoughts. Since you have been keeping such long vigil,
care seems to have made your forehead its abode.

SAUL: Oh, let me be, Madam! It is just because care
inhabits my brow that I must keep vigil thus. [*Guards
have entered. To the guards*] Well, what of the messengers?

FIRST GUARD: They are waiting for the King to call them.

SAUL: Where are they?

FIRST GUARD: In the courtyard.

SAUL: Among the people! [*Aside*] I should have done
this secretly.

QUEEN [*approaching*]:   Saul, my lord, is it true, as everyone in the palace is saying, that you have had the
prophets put to death?

SAUL: Not the prophets, Madam; the sorcerers. You
know very well that God does not tolerate them.

18

QUEEN: But who will tell the future for us now?

SAUL [*shouting*]:   The King! [*To the guards*] Come!
Have them called in!

[*Exit* GUARD, *left. Enter* JONATHAN, *right.* SAUL, *seeing
him:*]

Ah, here is Prince Jonathan. Good morning. I am
happy to see you with us at this hour. You will see how
a king should govern. It is time you should learn. Come
over here. [JONATHAN *to the* KING's *left, the* QUEEN *to
the right.*]

QUEEN [*leaning toward him*]:   Three more white hairs,
my lord! Barber, you are taking poor care of the King.
You must dress his hair again immediately after the
audience. His features look tired too, and his beard
unkempt. . . .

[*She has been moving toward the* BARBER. *Re-enter the*
GUARD.]

GUARD: My lord, the messengers are here.

KING: Send them in.

QUEEN [*to* BARBER, *in a low voice, as messengers enter*]:
Well, what?

BARBER: Madam, I have found someone! It is—

QUEEN: Tell me quickly. [*Their voices are covered.*]

KING: Eliphas! I entrusted the list to you.

ELIPHAS [*one of the messengers*]:   It is here. [*Handing
it to the* KING, *who examines it.*]

QUEEN [*to the* BARBER]:   David, you say?

BARBER: David, of Bethlehem.

KING [*reading*]:   Two at Ramah; the conjurer at Keilah;

19

three on Mount Bethel and four on Gilboa; at the well
of Sechu an interpreter of dreams; at Michmash . . .
[*He continues reading in a low voice. The* QUEEN *has
moved toward the* HIGH PRIEST; *when the* KING'S *voice
drops, the* QUEEN'S *can be heard.*]

QUEEN [*to the* HIGH PRIEST, *continuing*]:   David.

HIGH PRIEST: David?

QUEEN: Son of Jesse, yes, of Bethlehem. Go quickly and
have him sought for in the camp.

[*Exit the* HIGH PRIEST.]

SAUL: Tell me, now: it's true, you struck them from behind; or you struck from the front only those who were
asleep? So they could not see you? They didn't say
anything? [JONATHAN *reels.*] What! Jonathan—are you
faint?

JONATHAN: Why, no, Father. I am helping you govern.

SAUL: Lean on me; there! Be strong. . . . I cannot ask
that of everyone. (I am too weary this morning.) They
said nothing? . . . Ah! I told you to tear their tongues
out, every one of them.

ELIPHAS: We have the tongues.

SAUL [*to* JONATHAN]:   You see, some might talk after
death. [JONATHAN *faints.*] There now, he has fainted!
Ah! [*With an angry gesture*] Madam, take him off.
Fie! He's like a woman. He is making me do this
questioning very badly. . . . Now then, that's all, is
it? (I really am very tired.) They are all accounted
for. Every one—and not one spoke. If by chance one
of you heard anything, let him take care. . . . But,

verily, every one of you faithful servants will have his reward.

[*As he speaks, the* KING *passes his hand repeatedly over his forehead; takes off his crown. He rises and goes toward the door. Exeunt servants and messengers. The* FIRST GUARD *and the* BARBER *are left for a moment alone.*]

GUARD: What is the matter with the King? Is he sick?

BARBER: Never mind, never mind—I shall tend him.

GUARD: But—

[*Re-enter the* KING. *Seeing that the messengers have gone, he motions to the* GUARD.]

SAUL [*mysteriously*]:   Go and have those messengers killed. . . .

[*Exit the* GUARD.]

SCENE VIII

[THE BARBER, THE KING, THEN THE QUEEN]

BARBER [*to the* KING, *who moves away*]:   Will Your Majesty permit me—a slight freshening, a massage. . . . Oh! Oh! Even from a distance I could see that wrinkle—two strokes of this salve and it will be gone. [*Meanwhile he is taking his instruments from his case; seats the* KING *in a chair on the right.*]

And here are the gray hairs the Queen mentioned awhile ago. Ah, it's true they are a nice white; but the others are a nice black; and His Majesty has not yet

21

reached the age—His Majesty is marvelously well
preserved! [SAUL *gestures.*] Despite all the anxieties
of rule [SAUL *gestures again; the* BARBER *is putting
kohl under his eyes*]— Carefully! . . . To keep one's
handsome features . . . And yet! His Majesty has
wearied himself a trifle of late.

SAUL: I don't—

BARBER: No! No! Don't move the lips—I have made a
little slip in the beard. . . . Ah, I wanted to notify
His Highness; I have prepared something special, a
new kind of sherbet—with anise—yes, anise! It is most
particularly refreshing, and intoxicating! Ah! . . . If
His Majesty's thirst would do me the favor of requiring
it— And I was about to forget! How absent-minded!

[*Enter the* QUEEN *softly behind them.*]

The little singer I mentioned—

SAUL: You mentioned nothing of the kind.

BARBER: Mentioned nothing of the kind? Well, what
could I have been thinking of? A marvelous singer,
Sire—who accompanies himself on the harp.

SAUL: Well?

BARBER: Well, I have found him! [*With insinuation*]
He is here.

SAUL: But who asked you to—?

BARBER: Why, His Highness, His Highness—the other
day, getting out of his bath, His Highness exclaimed:
Ah! if there were only a little music! . . . But His
Highness is too weary now; he doesn't remember.

SAUL: Oh, that's enough of your harp-player! I want

22

no one, do you hear, no one around me. Just bring me your sherbet, I am thirsty.

QUEEN [*who has come close*]:   But do listen to him, my dear love. Such a nice guitar-player! My love, my heart; someone to play on the lyre and soothe your tired spirit a bit. . . .

SAUL: Well, if it isn't the Queen! If she is the one to propose it, it must be bad for me.

QUEEN: I have noticed that music and even war trumpets produce the best effect on your weakened faculties.

SAUL [*aside*]:   This woman detests me.

QUEEN: Often the mind may be charmed out of its anxiety by the song of a harp and give itself easily to sleep. . . .

SAUL [*aside*]:   I hate her. [*He rises.*]

QUEEN: Or, freed from its own impurity, it may find relief in incoherent speech that—

SAUL: Silence, Madam. I have heard quite enough from you.

[*Exit* SAUL.]

SCENE IX

[THE QUEEN, THE BARBER]

QUEEN: What now, barber!

BARBER: What else, Madam? We must give it up.

QUEEN: What! Are you discouraged? Bah! Let's keep
   trying; the King never knows what he wants. Wait
   until he sees him.

BARBER: Here he is.

[*Enter* DAVID *and the* HIGH PRIEST, *conversing.*]

SCENE X

[THE SAME, THEN THE HIGH PRIEST AND
            DAVID]

QUEEN: He is quite handsome.

HIGH PRIEST [*to someone off stage*]:   Fight with Goliath!
   It's ridiculous! [*They enter.*] Would you believe,
   Madam, that this child wanted—

QUEEN: I understand. But he is much too young.

BARBER: He's the one.

QUEEN: Hush! [*Exit the* BARBER.] Are you David? David
   of Bethlehem. Daoud, as some say.

DAVID [*pointedly*]:   David—yes, Madam.

QUEEN: I was looking for you, David.

DAVID: I was looking for you, Madam.

QUEEN [*angrily*]:   David! And why, David, were you
   looking for me?

DAVID: To ask you to let me fight.

QUEEN: The giant! Is this serious?

DAVID: What, Madam? The giant's challenge?

QUEEN: Yours, David.

DAVID: Do you doubt it?

QUEEN [*with a long look*]:   No. But you are a child, David. A mere child! How old?

DAVID: I am seventeen.

QUEEN: Seventeen! And you are a trained soldier?

DAVID: No. Until now I have lived in the mountains. I am a shepherd. I have never fought with men, but I have fought with bears that attacked my flock—bears and sometimes lions.

QUEEN [*to the* HIGH PRIEST]:   It's true he looks strong. [*To* DAVID] But they found you in the camp, you say? Why did you leave Bethlehem?

DAVID: Oh, a few days ago, for no reason, much. I was just going to see my brothers and carry them som honey cakes from my father that he had made for them. I am younger than they. They are in your army; but there's nobody in your army who wants to fight. They're all afraid. And they all laughed at me when I ılked about going against Goliath. They didn't want to let me [*angrily*] and my brothers even insulted me. That's why I wanted to come to you.

QUEEN: I shall not laugh at you, noble David.

DAVID: And you will let me?

QUEEN: Wait awhile.

HIGH PRIEST: What, Madam! Will you?

QUEEN: Let us try him. He pleases me. Nabal, do we have any armor?

HIGH PRIEST [*smiling*]:   The King's, Madam. It is no longer used.

25

QUEEN: Prince Jonathan cannot put it on.

HIGH PRIEST: Yes, but David is stronger.

QUEEN: Send for it. [*Following the* SERVANT *with her eyes as he exits*] Who was that who just went across the terrace? Wasn't it Prince Jonathan? Call him.

SCENE XI

[THE SAME, WITH JONATHAN]

QUEEN [*to* DAVID]:   This is Jonathan, my son; you will love him as a brother. Won't you, Jonathan? Now, children, embrace each other. [*To the* HIGH PRIEST] Look how sweet they are. Why, Prince Jonathan, you are smiling! I have never seen you smile before.

JONATHAN: I am smiling at David, Madam.

QUEEN: I see you are. He is going to fight.

JONATHAN: Goliath! Is it true, David?

[*The armor is brought in.*]

QUEEN: And here is the King's armor.

DAVID [*takes the helmet and puts it on for a moment; lifts the armor*]:   No! I shall fight as I am.

QUEEN: But this is madness, David.

DAVID: Excuse me, Madam; all this weight would not protect me so much as it would impede my courage. I am afraid of nothing, for I know the God of Israel protects me. I shall go as I am; with my sling, which I can handle easily.

26

[*The* SERVANT *who had brought the armor takes it away.*
The QUEEN *and the* HIGH PRIEST *look at each other.*]

HIGH PRIEST: Madam, let us leave it to him. He seems
brave indeed.

[*They move away slowly, but remain on stage.* DAVID
and JONATHAN *downstage.*]

JONATHAN: David, take my sling, will you?

DAVID [*takes it, examines it, gives it back*]:   I am used
to mine. It's better.

JONATHAN: Then take these stones.

DAVID [*same business*]:   They are not sharp enough.

QUEEN [*upstage*]:   Well, High Priest, come along! They
will get on together. Let's leave them alone. They are
children.

[*Exeunt.*]

JONATHAN: Then, what shall I give you, David? I should
like—

DAVID: Prince—

JONATHAN: Ah, don't call me Prince! Simply call me
Jonathan. Nobody here calls me Jonathan; it's always
Prince Jonathan! Even Father and Mother. I am sick
of it.

DAVID: My father and mother, at Bethlehem, call me
Daoud—but they're the only ones.

JONATHAN: Then what shall I call you?

DAVID: What they do: Daoud. Do you want to, Jonathan?

JONATHAN: You will conquer, Daoud! I'll watch you
from the top of the terrace.

27

ACT II

SCENE I

The scene is the same as in the first act, but fully lighted. The curtains, left, are raised. People are moving about forming animated groups. Enter JOEL *with the* BARBER, *right.*

FIRST MAN: I tell you, it was to see his brothers.

SECOND MAN: No, it was to fight the Philistines.

THIRD MAN: Come now! How could he have known, at Bethlehem? The Queen sent him to fight.

FOURTH MAN: Yes, when she saw him; but that doesn't explain how he got into the palace.

SECOND MAN: Did he get into the palace?

FOURTH MAN: Nor how he got to speak to the Queen.

FIRST MAN: He spoke to the Queen!

[*Enter another man.*]

FIFTH MAN: But listen! He would never have got to the King if the Queen had not been looking for a harp-player.

[*Enter another.*]

SIXTH MAN: He would never have got to the Queen if the King had not had a secret.

SECOND MAN: Ah! The King's secret! You want to know

the King's secret? [*He leans toward the first man and whispers.*]

FIRST MAN [*guffaws; then, to the third man*]: You want to know the King's secret? [*He whispers; the third man guffaws.*] Who wants to know the King's secret?

THIRD MAN: Ten drachmas for the King's secret!

[*During this speech enter another man.*]

SEVENTH MAN: All right! I too have a secret, like the King! [*They gather around him.*] Here it is: great Samuel, before he died, went to Bethlehem; he had little David brought to him, and in a little yard where almost no one saw him, he took some oil and anointed him, just as he had done for Saul. . . . That's thirty drachmas.

[JOEL *and the* BARBER *have approached.*]

JOEL: That secret might be worth a lot more, old blabber.

SEVENTH MAN: How much?

JOEL: Your head, you fool! Take care that no one—
[*All move away, disappear.*]

SEVENTH MAN: Ah, a man has small reward for his trust!

SCENE II

———————————

[JOEL AND THE BARBER]

JOEL: Does the King know this?

BARBER: Certainly not. Does the Queen?

JOEL [*threateningly*]:   Barber! Watch out. . . .

BARBER [*same business*]:   Joel! Take care. . . .

JOEL [*thinking better of it, suddenly congenial*]:   My good barber!

BARBER [*same business*]:   My excellent Joel! [*They join arms, about to leave. Shouting is heard off stage.*] Why all this shouting?

JOEL: David's escort passing.

[*Others join them, and all rush out. The shouting increases below the terrace.*]

BARBER: Hurry, let's go down.

[JONATHAN *and* SAKI *go toward the terrace.*]

SCENE III

———————————

[JONATHAN AND SAKI]

SAKI: No, this way, Prince; you can see better.

JONATHAN: Now, Saki, tell me again. All by himself!

With nothing but his sling! You saw him! Ah, how glorious he looked! He's my friend, you know. [*Saul enters.*] Come on, there's my father . . .

[*Exeunt. The stage remains empty for a moment.*]

SCENE IV

[SAUL]

SAUL [*pacing as he speaks*]:   I have won solitude!—because people avoid me. Come! Have this conqueror brought in to me. I am angry with him. I am very angry with everyone! Those yelling people exasperate me. Such acclamations—stolen from me—for an accidental triumph! They didn't acclaim me, for my difficult victories. . . . Ah, my good Queen, you choose your men well! A child, they tell me—why? To reassure me? Who gave him the right to conquer? You, perhaps! Not I. [*Continues to pace during the beginning of the following scene.* GUARDS *appear at the door, left.*]

SCENE V

[SAUL, DAVID, GUARDS]

SAUL: Come! Bring him to me. Heh! Why, this conqueror is a shepherd! It's true he's quite young. Ah, and
terribly handsome.

[*These three phrases are spoken in a lower and lower
voice.* SAUL, *striding across the stage, at first sees only*
DAVID's *back. He approaches him; then in a loud, angry
voice*]

His hands are still covered with blood! [*Looking him
over*] He is stained all over with it! He should have
cleansed himself before coming in! . . . You guards,
you should have warned him. Nothing bloody must
come in here! [DAVID *makes a move to leave.*] No! Let
him stay! Little giant killer, I am very angry with you.
[*He strides up and down. A short silence.*]

DAVID: Why are you angry with me, King Saul? It's true,
I won—but not against you.

SAUL: But who gave you permission?

DAVID: The Queen let—

SAUL: The Queen, yes. Listen, there is no queen in
Israel. There is only the King's wife.

DAVID [*after a silence*]:   Why are you angry, my lord?
It is to you that I am devoted.

32

SAUL [*aside*]:   Ah, his voice levels my anger as the rain of heaven a stir of dust! [*Aloud*] I would be left alone— [DAVID *is about to go*] with him.

[*Exeunt guards.*]

SCENE VI

———————

[DAVID AND THE KING]

SAUL [*continuing to pace*]:   I look quite angry, don't I? [DAVID *is silent.*] Come, speak! Tell me your name. What is your name?

DAVID: David.

SAUL: David—David. . . . The Moabites say Daoud. Do you want me to call you Daoud?

DAVID: No.

SAUL: No! Why? Let me call you— I want to call you Daoud.

DAVID: Someone already calls me that; I promised that only—

SAUL: Someone? Who? [DAVID *is silent.*] Shepherd, I want to know. I am your King.

DAVID: Your right goes only as far as your power.

SAUL: As my power? What do you do when one of the goats in your flock refuses to obey?

DAVID: I strike it.

SAUL: Do you still refuse?

DAVID: Strike me.

33

SAUL [*raising his spear, then changing his mind*]:   Do
   you love God?

DAVID: It is my love for Him that gives me strength.

SAUL: Are you so strong, David?

DAVID: He is very strong.

SAUL [*after a silence*]:   And what are you going to do
   now?

DAVID: I am going back to Bethlehem, my own country.

SAUL: No, David. Listen: I want to attach you to my
   person. . . . The Queen spoke to me of some harp-
   player; I do not want hers, but—

DAVID: She spoke of me.

SAUL [*concerned, then recovering*]:   Ah! So you can
   play. . . . But here is the Queen. Perhaps she was
   looking for you. I leave you. You will no doubt have
   matters to discuss.

[*He makes a move to leave, but hides behind a column.*]

SCENE VII

[THE QUEEN, DAVID, AND
SAUL, *concealed*]

Enter the QUEEN, *right, conversing with the* HIGH PRIEST.
Sees DAVID.

QUEEN [*to the* HIGH PRIEST]:   Here he is. Leave us.
[*Exit the* HIGH PRIEST.]

34

Ah! David! At last I have found you, covered with
glory, praise God! At first, though you were charming,
I saw in you only a shepherd; but now I wish to see
you only as a conqueror, glorious in your triumph.
What is your anxiety, David? You do look anxious. I
know the King spoke harshly to you awhile ago. Is
that it?

DAVID: No, Madam; he gradually softened the sharpness
of his words, and after a while spoke very gently to me.

QUEEN: And for a long time, too. You were alone together, weren't you?

DAVID: Yes, for a while.

SAUL [*concealed*]:   They are too far. I can hear nothing.

QUEEN: You would be quite wrong, David, to worry
about such things. The King's humor must not vex
you, it is no great matter; he is harsh and often hostile
for no reason, and constantly changing.

DAVID: But I am not at all worried about it, Madam. The
King was very kind to me.

QUEEN: I am glad of that, David. It's true, your beauty
could only please him; but the good you speak of the
King will help our affairs greatly. For I wish you well,
David. The courage you have shown deserves a better
reward than the ovations of a stupid and excited people. . . . I see that you can talk to the King; his bad
humor changed when he talked with you, and— But
first, David, listen: do not forget you owe this honor
to me!

DAVID: What honor, Madam?

35

QUEEN: Of being singer to the King.

DAVID: Excuse me, Madam, but I had already heard—

QUEEN: Ah! The high priest told you?

DAVID: No.

QUEEN: The barber?

DAVID: The King himself also, asked me—

QUEEN: Ah!

DAVID: This seems to make you angry?

QUEEN: Why angry, David? On the contrary, isn't it all to the good that we have both found in you what we desire? And what did you answer?

[*They are drawing near the* KING.]

DAVID: It was just then that you came in, and the King left before I could answer him.

[*Still nearer.*]

QUEEN: Then, answer—now.

DAVID: But the King is no longer here, Madam.

SAUL [*concealed*]:   Good! Courageous David!

QUEEN: David, your youth needs instruction. King Saul does not have the authority you suppose.

SAUL [*concealed*]:   Ah! Ah!

QUEEN: I know he used to be a King full of wisdom and courage; but now his will has overreached itself, and needs to be directed; it is I, often, who make his decisions. As you see, the idea of keeping a singer with him is mine. He is willing and I'm glad, since the singer is to be yourself. But you must understand also, David, that the King is sick with evil fancies; he needs me to watch over him constantly.

SAUL [*concealed*]: Have a care, Madam.

QUEEN: But he tells me little; I am rarely with him. . . . Every least word, his slightest gesture, everything he does may throw some light on his illness and teach me to take wiser care of him. You must report everything to me.

DAVID: Madam!

QUEEN: David, you must not mistake my words. Without my care what would become of your King? You will help me. Together we may sometimes soothe away his troubles. You will know sooner than I what they are, and you will tell me. Then the two of us— Why don't you say something? Answer me. . . . Ah, for a conqueror you seem far too timid! And you lower your eyes just when I am raising mine—on you—Daoud. But so charming. [*She touches his cheek with her hand.*]

DAVID: Ah! Madam! The King—

[SAUL *springs from behind the column.* DAVID *runs away. Exit.*]

SCENE VIII

———————

[SAUL, THE QUEEN]

———————

SAUL: Daoud! Enough, Madam, enough! You can see very well that this child— Come back, David! I will

37

not harm you, David. See! You are not the one to be
punished.

[*He seizes the* QUEEN *by her hair and garments and drags
her to the floor.*]

QUEEN: Is this jealousy? . . . You!

SAUL: Ah, do not trifle, Madam. . . . I am jealous, terribly!

[*He stabs her several times with his spear.*]

QUEEN: Detestable Saul! I was too rash to hate you
deeply enough! May the whole weight of your crown
now fall on you alone! Keep your cares to yourself.
Guard them! Dangerous King Saul! Henceforth be
dangerous to yourself. I shall see whether you can hide
your secret from the dead. . . . I didn't know it was so
dreadful.

[*She dies.*]

SAUL [*leaning over the* QUEEN]:   You are wrong, Madam. The secret you would find is another. . . .

SCENE IX

---

*The scene is in Saul's bedchamber, which is poorly lit
with a single smoky lamp. No furniture. On the right, a
bed. On the left, a window. Near the center, a sort of
throne with benches to right and left, or at any rate some
means of sitting beside the throne.* KING SAUL *is dressed*

as formerly in his purple mantle; he wears the crown.

SAUL [*going to the door, closing it with care*]:   Ah! Night
has been long in coming. . . . [*He draws a curtain
over the door, turns around, looks about him.*] And now
that I am alone . . . [*He sits.*]

CHORUS OF DEMONS [*surging out, they sit quickly on the
floor in a circle before him. Their voices join with
SAUL's, saying*]:   Let's take counsel!

SAUL [*still not seeing them*]:   It is quieter here than on
the terrace. And Saki asked to stay with Jonathan this
evening. . . .

A DEMON [*finishing his sentence*]:   —and David.

SAUL: Yes. Anyway, I wanted to be alone. . . . The
smell of flowers bothered me out there; and I can no
longer see anything in the stars, I don't even look at
them any more.

FIRST DEMON: When he starts talking to himself, you
know it's not going to be funny!

[*He yawns; others stretch.*]

SAUL [*continuing*]:   Maybe the sorcerers—

SECOND DEMON: He's going on just as if we were not
here.

SAUL: Maybe they saw something.

THIRD DEMON: We are going to have to break in.

SAUL: What did they know? I should have spared several and kept them with me.

FOURTH DEMON: He won't let us get in a word.

FIRST DEMON: Patience!

SAUL [*staring at the demons, without seeing them*]: Here my thought stops, stands fixed on one point, and yet I do not know what point.

FIFTH DEMON: You could risk a few trial propositions.

SAUL: It seems to me that my attention is fixed, but on what, I do not know.

SIXTH DEMON: Then it must be on David.

SAUL: They want to know my secret; but do I know it myself? I have several.

FIRST DEMON: With us, you know, there's no need to be bashful.

SAUL: I understand now why I cared so little for the Queen. It was too easy for me to practice chastity in my youth. I practiced a great many virtues. . . . Ah, I wanted to congratulate myself on getting rid of the Queen—and study the advantages. . . .

SEVENTH DEMON: You could also—

SAUL: That's what I told myself—get rid of the high priest too. . . . There are more questions in Israel than he has answers for. When I have questions to ask, I don't ask him. There are more answers in heaven than questions on the lips of men.

SEVENTH DEMON: But—

SAUL: . . . some answers are a long time coming.

THIRD DEMON [*together with the* FOURTH]: Or cannot be seen.

FOURTH DEMON: We make them ourselves.

[*The two demons jump at one another and fight. But for*

a moment only. Nothing in the course of the scene is disturbed.]

FIRST DEMON: Ah! Come on, King Saul! Talk to us!

SAUL: He claims to love God, and says his strength comes only from Him. I would willingly love God myself; I did love Him; but He has forsaken me. Why?

FIRST DEMON: So that we could come nearer.

[*They laugh.*]

SAUL: My eyes fall shut, from weariness and misery.

FIFTH DEMON: You need a little to drink.

SAUL: Do you think so? No—not yet. Anyway, Saki is not here.

SECOND DEMON: But we are, we're here.

SAUL: Ah, faithful friends.

SECOND DEMON: Ah, come on, now! Old Saul! This is surely the least you can say.

THIRD DEMON: King Saul, you are thirsty.

SAUL: Yes, it's true. I'm going to get my cup.

FIFTH DEMON: Why, no, old King! Wait until it is brought to you.

FIRST DEMON: Oh, let him go. It gives him something to do.

[*The two fight. KING SAUL rises. This should be played as if he were continuing a monologue. He seems tottering with indecision. The sound of fighting increases.*]

SAUL: Not so much racket, children! I can't even hear myself.

SECOND DEMON: You're not saying anything.

[*They all writhe with laughter.* SAUL *cannot keep from laughing also, despite himself.*]

SAUL [*grasping the cup and the jug of wine, takes a small swallow*]: . . . And the jug. Ah, this crown bothers me. . . . [*He throws it onto his bed from some distance and returns to his seat. His robes slip down a little from his shoulders. He sits down, drinks another swallow; then, seeing the demons:*] Why, my young friends, you must be very uncomfortable on the floor! Come sit here beside me.

[*All jump up and sit beside* SAUL.]

FIRST DEMON: Oh, it's for your convenience, you know, not for ours.

[SAUL *smiles.*]

SECOND DEMON [*pretending to take* SAUL's *smile for an invitation*]:   Closer?

SAUL [*choking slightly*]:   You are smothering me a bit.

FOURTH DEMON: Oh no! Oh no! It's because you need a drink.

FIFTH DEMON: Shall I pour it? Hurry; the night will soon be gone.

[SAUL *holds his cup; the* DEMON *fills it.* SAUL *empties it.*] Another?

[SAUL *holds out his cup again. The* DEMON *fills it. As* SAUL *carries it to his lips*]

SEVERAL DEMONS: But what about us?

[SAUL *lowers his cup a little. The* DEMONS *crowd upon him, each trying to take the cup. They knock it over.*]

SAUL [*rises abruptly, rolling the* DEMONS *to the floor,*

*where they remain. He lets the cup fall, and in a loud
voice*]:   Ah! You have stained my robe!

[*He now paces, or stands motionless; the lamp dies, and
a glimmer of dawn begins to whiten the window on the
left. But the stage remains still quite dark. A rather long
silence.*]

SECOND DEMON [*in a very different tone of voice*]:   Saul!
Saul! Now is the hour when the herdsmen are driving
their flocks from the stables.

THIRD DEMON: Saul! You could climb up now to the
tower, and watch the coming dawn.

FOURTH DEMON: Or on the sweet-smelling hillside, in
the pure morning air, you could sing, sing a canticle.

FIFTH DEMON: The grasses are bathed in dew. . . .

SIXTH DEMON: The baths are ready in the palace.

FIRST DEMON: Oh! What I should find most delightful,
after a sleepless night, is a sherbet of anise with a
liqueur.

SEVENTH DEMON: As for me, I should rather hear David
sing.

[*They all laugh.*]

SAUL [*taking his head in his hands*]:   To be alone! Alone!
[*He opens the window, a bit of dawn enters, he falls to
his knees, lifting his hands toward the open air. The* DE-
MONS *gradually disappear, without flourish.*]

God of David! Help me!

ACT III

SCENE I

The scene is the same as in the first act, except that the curtains separating the hall from the terrace, upstage left, are drawn. JOEL, *entering left, is about to cross the stage. The* BARBER *lifts the curtain.*

BARBER: Psst! Joel!

JOEL: Oh, it's you, barber.

BARBER: Have you seen David?

JOEL: That's for you to say. I don't know him.

BARBER [*disclaiming*]: I know him very slightly!

JOEL: No matter; it's up to you. Be careful, barber, be careful.

BARBER: Let's both be careful, Joel! Let's both be careful.

[*Silence. The* BARBER *begins to weep.*]

The Queen was careful too!

JOEL: She was too careful.

BARBER [*weeping*]: Poor lady! Everything was going so well with her.

[*Silence.*]

JOEL: This little David is astonishing; all he had to do was appear—

44

BARBER: To clean the place out.

JOEL: To get it cleaned out, you mean.

BARBER: I'd rather help clean than—

JOEL: Yes—but remember, Saul is doing the cleaning.

BARBER: One's interests are rather—complex. Whom is one to serve! Great heaven! Whom? All I ask is to devote myself! . . . You can't be too careful.

JOEL: Let's do be careful, barber, do be careful! . . . But where the devil did you get the notion that the King has no will of his own?

BARBER: Ah, I beg your pardon! I did not say that; I said his will was sick; it works in spurts.

JOEL: Be careful that it doesn't spurt on us! Huh! A will like that is more to be feared than any. His decisions seem to have no motive. Be careful of the King, barber.

BARBER: If you think that's easy. The high priest—

JOEL: What?

BARBER: Well, he chatters now when he talks to the King.

JOEL: What do you mean: he chatters?

BARBER: I mean his teeth chatter, for fear of the King. [JOEL *shrugs his shoulders.*] And Saul is very difficult to approach lately. Besides, everybody leaves when he comes in. And he is always spying; he hides. You never hear him coming; and then you catch him, behind a curtain, listening. Or he catches you. And everybody scuttles noiselessly from room to room through the palace, where you know the King too is prowling noiselessly. . . .

45

JOEL [*during the* BARBER'*s speech, has gone to the drawn curtain on the left and with a large abrupt gesture lifts it*]:   The devil!

BARBER [*startled by the noise*]:   Ah, how you frightened me! You know I have no sword.

JOEL: Never mind, barber, you will speak to the King; and whatever you learn—

BARBER [*eying Joel's sword*]:   It's wonderful, Joel, how close our friendship is becoming!

JOEL: Everything serves to— [*He ends with a gesture of fastening his sword belt.*]

BARBER [*fitting words to Joel's gesture*]:   —bind us closer. Well! Here is David! Hurry! Leave us.

[DAVID *crosses the terrace. Exit* JOEL.]

SCENE II

———————————

[DAVID AND THE BARBER]

BARBER [*mysteriously*]:   Prince David! . . . Prince David!

DAVID: What is it, barber?

BARBER [*breathless*]:   I have been running after you for the last four days without finding you for one moment alone, Prince David!

DAVID: I am not a prince, barber.

BARBER: Yes, my lord, but—

46

DAVID [*more and more severe*]:   Nor a lord, either.

BARBER: I do not know what name to give to the glorious conqueror who—

DAVID: It was only by God's help that I conquered, **bar**ber! I am not even a captain of the army.

BARBER: But your courage—

DAVID: It's no greater than my faith.

BARBER: Exactly: faith. . . . But your hope for the future—

DAVID: My only hope is that the God of Israel, who called me to kill Goliath, will now be content and let me go back to Bethlehem, to my father, and keep his goats, as before.

BARBER: Oh, goats! My lord David should dream of being a keeper of men; and that is exactly what I wanted to say to him—quickly, before someone comes. You know that King Saul is sick, and that Jonathan is weak as some rare little bird; you know that neither of them any longer has popular favor, and that, if my prince so desired, I, the King's doctor, and barber, with him every day, I could—

DAVID: Now that you have told me your secret, barber, listen to the one I shall tell you: I love Saul as my King, and Jonathan more than myself; I fear God, barber, and you would do better to watch your words lest they offend His chosen one. You called me prince a moment ago. It must have been because you want me to order you to do something, barber. Well, get out!

[*Exit* BARBER.]

47

Jonathan! Jonathan! May the Eternal set firmly on
your feeble brow this tottering royalty! . . .
[*Enter* SAUL *and* JONATHAN.]

SCENE III

[SAUL, JONATHAN, DAVID]

SAUL *is in common clothes,* JONATHAN *dressed in all the
insignia of royalty.* DAVID *has stepped back into the corner, left; without seeing him,* SAUL *and* JONATHAN *ad-
vance toward the throne.* SAUL *notices that the curtain
has been lifted and lets it down again with special care.*

SAUL: This is how I like to see you, Jonathan. Come!
Take my place this evening on the throne. It is time
that you should practice ruling, even in an empty hall.
Consciousness of one's royalty is greatly fortified by the
habit of its insignia. Learn to bear them. The other day
when the messengers came, I think you would not have
fainted, despite the added weight of the crown, had
you been sitting on the royal throne, sustained by the
scepter and the pride of the purple in which you are
robed today.

JONATHAN: Oh, Father, let me alone; I am so tired! If
you knew how heavy this crown is!

SAUL: Ah, so! Do you think I do not know? . . . It is
just for this reason that you should begin, now, to get

accustomed to it. I am old; and the less steadily it sits
upon my head, the more becoming of you to hold it
steady on yours.

JONATHAN: Father! No more! My head aches. . . .
Take your royalty.

SAUL: No! No! Wear it until tonight . . . Naturally, I
shall put it on again to sleep. . . . But for the moment,
stay as you are, robed in purple, and so long as no one
comes in, just imagine that you are reigning over thou-
sands. [DAVID *stirs. To* JONATHAN] Ah, you are indeed
a ruler! [*To* DAVID] I didn't expect you until somewhat
later, David. But never mind, stay. Yes, the young King
is trying himself out. I thought that for this evening
there would be no one for him to rule, but here you
are. So farewell; I leave you with His Royal Highness.
[SAUL *moves away to the right. Aside*] I'm glad he saw
me without my crown; it made him too distant and
respectful.

[*Exit.* DAVID *and* JONATHAN *wait motionless for* SAUL *to
be gone.*]

SCENE IV

[JONATHAN, DAVID, THEN SAUL, *concealed*]

JONATHAN: Daoud!

DAVID: Ah, my young, triumphant King! How beautiful

49

you are in your glory! Why are you not Saul? Why was
it not for you that I was called, to sing for you more
beautiful songs! Or just to be with you and gaze on you
in silence! Or throw myself at your feet, as I do now.
[*Then rising, laughing, he runs to* JONATHAN *and embraces him.*]

SAUL [*lifting the drapes on the left*]:   Slow, there! Not
too fast!

JONATHAN: Why do you laugh, David, when I am horribly pale, and you see I am going to cry? A bit more
and I should be falling at your feet, with fatigue.

DAVID [*stepping back*]:   Jonathan!

JONATHAN [*rising, coming forward*]:   Just feel the
weight of this crown. How heavy, eh?

SAUL [*concealed*]:   A good lookout post. Oh!

JONATHAN [*handing the crown to* DAVID]:   Look how
it bruised my forehead. David, I am sick. . . . Isn't it
heavy, though? . . . Oh say, put it on! [*He sets it on*
DAVID's *head.*]

SAUL: Oh, I shouldn't have seen that. . . .

JONATHAN: How well it suits you! But say, isn't it
heavy?

SAUL: Oh, David! So? It might be you—

DAVID: Poor Jonathan! To please you, I should like to
find it heavier. How weak you must be!

JONATHAN: It's true, it doesn't look heavy now, on your
forehead—Daoud.

SAUL: It might be you! Jonathan! [*Falls to his knees,
sobbing, half wrapping himself in the curtain.*]

DAVID: But you are ill, aren't you, Jonathan? You are pale, and perspiring. . . .

JONATHAN: These robes are smothering me. . . . This girdle—this sword is dragging me down; I can still feel the crown's weight on my forehead. Ah, Daoud! I'd like to throw off all this royalty. . . . I'd like to stretch out on the ground and sleep. . . . Ah, why am I not like you, a herdsman, bare but for a sheepskin—always in the open air. How handsome you are, David! I should like to walk in the mountains with you. You would move every stone from my path; at noon we'd bathe our tired feet in the cool water, and lie down among the vines. You would sing, and I'd tell you, far too much, of my love.

SAUL [*who has followed this speech as if he were saying it himself*]:   Yes.

JONATHAN: Night would come; and since you are strong —here, take the sword—you would defend me against the wild beasts. I should lie down, with your strength beside me! Ah, I am choking! Here, you put on the royal robes. Undo this cloak. [*He helps* DAVID, *who disrobes him.*]

SAUL: Ah, I ought not—to see.

JONATHAN: Under this purple your shoulder looks whiter. . . . Now my girdle.

SAUL: Ah, I cannot— I am suffering martyrdom.

JONATHAN: I cannot tell whether it's from joy, or the cold, or the effects of fever, or from love, but I am shivering in my simple tunic.

SAUL: How handsome he is in purple! Daoud! [*as if calling to him in a low voice.*]

DAVID: Jonathan! You are more beautiful in your white tunic than in all your royal ornaments. I did not know how elegant you are, what grace your weakness gives to your body.

SAUL: Ah!

DAVID: Jonathan, it was for your sake that I came down from the mountains; up there in the too ardent sun your fragile flower would have faded. You're weeping! Shall I weep too, with tenderness? You're trembling? Are you faint? Come, your frailty will find comfort in my arms.

SAUL: Ah, no! Not that—not that. . . .

JONATHAN [*swooning*]: Daoud!

SAUL [*staggering in, as if mad; aloud*]: But Saul, eh? Eh, Saul?

JONATHAN [*frightened*]: Go, David, quickly!

[*When* SAUL *appears,* DAVID *quits* JONATHAN, *sadly, and leaves, not too quickly, throwing off the royal garments with horror behind him.* JONATHAN *falls in a swoon.*]

DAVID: Horrible! Horrible!

SAUL: Eh, Saul? [*Stupefied and without a word, he watches* DAVID *vanish; approaches* JONATHAN, *kneels beside him, and takes his arm.*] He is too thin! . . . Come, Jonathan—speak to me. Don't you know me? I frightened you, I know, but I don't detest you. . . . [*In disgust, letting go the arm he was holding*] Ah, weaker than a woman! [*Leaning over him*] Is it your love for David that makes you pale? [*He runs to the right, calling*] David! He is still going. As if he were the one to be afraid! [*He runs left, lifts the curtain, calls.*] Ho! Come, someone! Help, someone!

CURTAIN

SCENE V

SAUL's *bedchamber.* SAUL *enters, conversing with the* HIGH PRIEST.

SAUL: So, not a single one is left; not even the least sorcerer?

HIGH PRIEST: His Majesty surely knows that they have all been done away with, according to his orders.

SAUL: That is not what I am asking you! I want to know whether perhaps some unimportant one has not been forgotten.

HIGH PRIEST: Not a single one.

SAUL: Understand me, it is not that I mean to punish the oversight—on the contrary—I wish one had been forgotten. . . . I need one—myself.

HIGH PRIEST: [*Silent.*]

SAUL: Oh well, you may go. [*Exit the* HIGH PRIEST.] What's to be done? Nothing! Nothing! The least soothsayer would know better than I. [*Running suddenly to the door*] Ah! High Priest! High Priest! [*Re-enter the latter.*] Your God? Is He still silent?

53

HIGH PRIEST: Still silent.

SAUL: This is too much! What have I done to Him?
Come, tell me, priest! Why is He silent? You must
explain, after all. . . . Ah, I wanted to justify myself
before Him. I am the accused; you, my judge: question me.

HIGH PRIEST [*struck dumb with terror*]:   What?

SAUL [*aside*]:   How stupid! [*To the* HIGH PRIEST] How
do I know! Ask me whether I have lived with heathen
women.

HIGH PRIEST: Yes.

SAUL: What, yes? I tell you to ask me whether I have
taken to myself any heathen women. Ask me, you
wretch, or I'll— [*brandishing his spear*].

HIGH PRIEST [*trembling*]:   I ask you whether you have
lived with any heathen women?

SAUL: No: I have not lived with any heathen women!
Do you hear? You know very well I've not lived with
any heathen women. [*Suddenly calm*] Come! Quick!
Ask me another.

HIGH PRIEST: What else?

SAUL: Ask me—you must know what! There are many
little commandments—

HIGH PRIEST: There are the Ten Commandments.

SAUL: Well! Say your Ten Commandments. What are
you waiting for? Come.

HIGH PRIEST [*reciting*]:   I am the Lord thy God, which
have brought thee out of the land of Egypt, out of the
house of bondage.

54

SAUL: And hurry up, I'm expecting the barber.

HIGH PRIEST: Thou shalt have no other gods before me.

SAUL: No, not that way. Ask me them.

HIGH PRIEST: Hast thou made unto thee any graven image or likeness of any thing that is in the heaven above, or that is in the earth beneath, or that is in the water under the earth? [SAUL *shrugs his shoulders with impatience.*] Hast thou bowed thyself to them or served them? For I the Lord thy God am a jealous God [SAUL *yawns*], visiting the iniquity of the fathers upon the children unto the third and fourth generation of them that hate Me, and—

SAUL [*relieved*]: Ah, here is the barber. You will go on with that another time. [*Exit the* HIGH PRIEST.]

SCENE VI

[SAUL; THE BARBER]

SAUL: Here you are, my sweet barber! Light the torches; we can't see in here.

[*The* BARBER *lights the torches, lays out his instruments.*]

[*Aside*] I should like to be sure that it's not David I have to fear! I cannot—I cannot hate him. I want him to like me! [*The* BARBER *motions that he is ready.*] I have called you in to cut off my beard.

BARBER [*stunned with surprise*]: Cut off your beard!

55

SAUL: Yes, my beard. It makes me look much older. It's time now for me to look a little younger. . . . That will make me look younger, won't it?

BARBER: Unquestionably! But you will look less respectable.

SAUL: I don't want to look too respectable. Come, are you ready? I'm waiting!

BARBER: But, indeed, does the King really mean what he says?

SAUL: Now, now, barber! Do I look as if I were joking? [*He laughs.*] Yes, but you will see how much better I can joke without my beard. Come! Seriously, cut it off.

BARBER [*beginning the operation*]:   And yet such a beautiful beard! It's a pity.

SAUL: Bah! It hid my face. A king must be able to make sudden decisions. How do I look, barber, eh?

BARBER: Tired.

SAUL: Ah!

BARBER: One can see that His Majesty works a great deal.

SAUL: Yes; I had to work all night again.

BARBER: Ah, now that the Queen is no longer here, His Majesty must be much more occupied with important affairs of the kingdom.

SAUL: There are more important affairs than those of the kingdom—and they concern no one but me.

BARBER: Oh, yes!

SAUL: What?

BARBER: I said: Oh, yes! I mean: Oh, yes. That is, cer-

tainly they concern no one but the King—and that is
why he is so tired, always obliged to keep everything
to himself. Perhaps also His Majesty feels too much
anxiety over certain things; it's true that if the Philistines—

SAUL: The Philistines?

BARBER [*continuing*]:   —come back.

SAUL: Ah—come back!

BARBER: The King is aware that people are saying they
will come back.

SAUL: He knows, he knows; but—

BARBER: But—if I dared say so—the King needs a
sorcerer?

SAUL: Ah! So you know—

BARBER: Ye—es.

SAUL: How?

BARBER: What does it matter?

SAUL: Do you know—

BARBER: Shsht! Oh, my scissors [*dropping them*]! Shsht!
One moment! There now! Un-rec-og-niz-able! I have
made the King look ten years younger.

SAUL [*anxious*]:   Tell me! Do you know one?

BARBER: Ye—es.

SAUL: A sorcerer?

BARBER: No, a sorceress.

SAUL: Where?

BARBER: At Endor.

SAUL: Ah! The witch of Endor! How had I forgotten
her?

BARBER: What! You know her too?

SAUL: She is the one who talks to the dead. Yes, I saw
her once, long ago; I had forgotten her. I had strangely
forgotten her. . . . But she knows me. So you say I am
unrecognizable?

BARBER: The King may take the mirror: I have finished.

SAUL: Yes—I'm not bad so! . . . Oh, that wrinkle!

BARBER: Your beard hid it a little. May I try?

SAUL: No; leave it. And go. [*Exit the* BARBER.] Unrecognizable! For once my passion serves my interest.
I shall go. [*Goes and opens the window.*] The sky is
heavy. A frightful storm is coming up. All the desert
sand is stirred and rising. No matter! [*Leaves the window, takes off his robes, puts on an old cloak.*] Unrecognizable indeed! [*As if repeating a lesson*] There
is someone I must beware of. [*Kneeling*] My God, let
it not be David! I cannot—I cannot— [*Rises.*] Bah!
It is too long since I tried to pray. And even when I
could pray, it was the same. Let it be a struggle between us. It is not up to me to come back; he forsook
me first. But I should like to be sure—that it is not he.
[*Wind from the window blows the torches.*] Ah, the
wind! Come!

[*Exit* SAUL.]

SCENE VII

The scene is inside a small cave; the entrance is upstage,
left; to the right a fireplace casts a glimmering light.

[T H E   W I T C H ,   T H E N   K I N G   S A U L]

WITCH OF ENDOR: Four pieces of bread, a few roots, and
then, prophetess of Endor, source of the only foresight
left in Israel, you will be used up, extinguished, like a
dying flame. The people from whom I beg think they
are good to me because they do not denounce me to the
King; they don't denounce me, but neither do they give
me any more to eat. King Saul! Why did you have us
all murdered? And yet do you remember one day when
you were the son of Kish, still uncrowned, the keeper
of your father's flocks, you came to me; you were
searching the desert in vain for a few stray asses; it was
that day I predicted, and I was the first, that you would
be King. And ever since that day, King Saul, people
claim that you are a prophet! What are your proph-
ecies? Do your lips tremble, like mine, that cannot
close on the horrible pressure of the future? What
future transpires through you, that you should wish
to be the only one to know it? That you should mas-
sacre the soothsayers? Ah, let them be hushed in the
tomb! But you, King Saul, will you be hushed? As for

59

me, I am used up, I will go. Men once would come thirsting for the unknown, and lean over my lips, streaming prophecy like the borders of a fountain. And men have not loved me; they wanted me to predict happy things, but my predictions were beyond happiness. And now I think it is not good for man to know the future, for no joy of man can last longer than it takes to say: "I am happy"; and he must be quick to say even that; for he has all the rest of time to say: "I *was* happy." The happiness of man is blind. . . .

I am cold. What frightful weather! All the toads around have come into my cave for shelter; the rain is pouring, and the wind blows so cold I thought it would kill me before I died of hunger. Never did I feel so faint. Who could be so tormented by the future that he would set out in such weather? Three times I doubted, but the fourth time the flame repeated the sign: someone is coming. I thought I was quite forgotten. Let's get ready to receive. Now, O last torch of Israel, let's cast a dying glimmer of light for the approaching stranger! And then let the curtain fall, now raised for the last time. And let the open mouths of the dead be closed on their secret, forever—forever! Ah! Ah! Ah! He is coming.

[*The* WITCH, *kneeling, now leans over the caldron, from which vapors seem to rise; she shakes her head and body and speaks in a manner more and more breathless and inspired. The water in the caldron is her mirror, in which she seems to see all that she recounts in her monologue.*]

The stranger is coming—he knows the way—not even carrying a torch. . . . Falling on me, ah, I feel the weariness of his journey—up the mountain! Ah, his journey! He slips in the muddy path—of the mountain. The wind blows—through his cloak. Weariness. Ah, I must be dying now! A poor, wretched old woman, old as the world's cares, let her die and not be disturbed. . . . He is coming! The stranger is coming! Ah, how the briars are tearing him! His head is bare: he looks as mortally weary as myself—wretched, ah, wretched as myself. He falls to his knees. Ah, let him pray! No, he's up, running, running down the path to the cave; a spear in his hand—oh, pity me. My strength is gone; I hear his steps. Here! Here!

[*The sorceress, more and more haggard, raises her head. At the word "here" she looks around her, showing that the two sources of her vision, the real and the imaginary, have come together.*]

Am I dying? [*In a louder and louder voice, ending in a cry*] Pity me! Pity! Pity! [*Enter* SAUL.] Saul!

SAUL [*on the threshold of the cave, dressed in a rough homespun cloak, badly torn; he looks haggard; his hair, streaming with rain, over his face. In despair*]: Ah! You recognize me? But I do not look like a king!

WITCH [*face to the ground*]: Pity me, Saul! Pity poor wretched me.

SAUL: Am I any less wretched than you?

WITCH: Pity, Saul! I am dying. . . .

SAUL: Do not be afraid of me, Pythonissa! I have not

61

come to try you. I have come to beg of you, and not
for you to beg of me. . . . [*He takes his head in his
hands.*] My distress is unbearable.

WITCH: Is this King Saul speaking so?

SAUL: Yes, it is Saul. No, not the King. Ah, why,
Pythonissa, why did you predict that I would be King?
Do you remember how handsome I was without a
crown? Any shepherd in the hills (and I was one!)
has more royalty in his stride than I have with all my
crown and purple robes! I know one who rules all,
wherever he goes. . . . But I— [*sitting wearily on a
stone*] am worn out.

WITCH [*rising, speaking in condolence, unable to find
words*]:   Saul—the way was hard, in this weather.

SAUL: This weather! Is it raining? [*Feeling his wet
cloak*] Yes, I am cold! Come closer to me; I need com-
forting.

WITCH [*touching* SAUL's *forehead with great tenderness*]:
Saul!

SAUL: What?

WITCH: Nothing. I pity you, King Saul.

SAUL: Ah! Pity? . . . It's true, I need pity—Pythonissa!
Night after night now— [*Seems to slump in his seat.*]
Ah, I am faint! Night after night I have been seeking,
wearing my soul out seeking. . . .

WITCH: Seeking what—the future? Saul.

SAUL [*prophetically*]:   The unspeakable torment of my
soul! . . . [*Recovering*] I am weaker than usual to-

night; some days I seem reasonably well, but the journey up here has finished me. I ate nothing tonight.

WITCH: I have a little bread—do you want some?

SAUL: No; not yet; my soul is hungrier than my body. Tell me, Pythonissa: can you raise the dead?

WITCH [*troubled*]:   The dead—is that what you want? Who?

SAUL: Who? Samuel.

WITCH [*frightened*]: He is too great!

SAUL: Am I Saul?

WITCH: You will be obeyed. You still know how to command. [*She approaches the fire and makes certain gestures and signs for raising the dead.*] See, the flame is quivering already. Stand back.

SAUL [*standing, holding his cloak over his face so as not to see the apparition, but not hiding himself from the audience*]:   Samuel! Samuel! Samuel! I have come. I call upon you, but fear your dreadful apparition. Speak to me! Let your words strike me—strike me down or comfort me; I am drained with uncertainty. My anxiety is harder to bear than any word of yours. Pythonissa! Pythonissa! What do you see?

WITCH: Nothing yet.

SAUL: I dare not look. . . . My soul is light and leaping within me, as if I were going to sing. I am faint. Pythonissa! Pythonissa! What do you see?

WITCH: Nothing. . . . Ah! Ah! Ah! I see a god ascending out of the earth.

63

SAUL: What shape does he take?

WITCH: An old man coming up; he is covered with a
mantle.

SAUL [*bowing down*]:   Samuel!

GHOST OF SAMUEL: Why did you disturb me in my sleep?

SAUL: I am sore distressed; for the Philistines make war
against me—and God has forsaken me.

GHOST OF SAMUEL: Wherefore ask of me, seeing the
Lord is departed from you and is become your enemy?

SAUL: Whom then could I ask, if not you? God answers
me no more, neither by his priests nor in dreams. Who
is to tell me what I must do now?

GHOST OF SAMUEL: Saul! Saul! Why do you always lie
before God? You know well that from the bottom of
your heart another thought arises; it is not the Philistines that trouble you. That is not why you have come
to question me.

SAUL: Speak, then, Samuel; you know my secret better
than I do myself. Fear has assailed my soul on every
hand; I no longer dare to look into my thought. Tell
me what it is.

GHOST OF SAMUEL: Saul! Saul! There are other enemies
than the Philistines to be put down; but you have taken
to your heart the very thing that harms you.

SAUL: I will submit—

GHOST OF SAMUEL: It is too late, Saul; God is now the
protector of your enemy. Even before he was conceived in his mother's womb, God had chosen him for

64

Himself. It is to prepare yourself for this that you have taken the enemy to your heart.

SAUL: But what was my error?

GHOST OF SAMUEL: To have received him.

SAUL: But God had chosen him.

GHOST OF SAMUEL: Do you think that God did not foresee, long ago, the final faltering of your soul and decide to punish you? He has posted your enemies before your gates; they hold your punishment in their hands; they wait at your half-closed gates, but they were long ago invited in. In your heart you feel impatient with their waiting: you know very well that what you call fear is really desire.

Listen to me: the Philistines you spoke of are now ready. God will deliver all Israel into their hands. [SAUL *falls full-length to the ground.*] Your royalty will be like a bit of torn purple, like water running through the half-closed fingers of your hand. . . .

SAUL [*sighing*]:   But Jonathan?

GHOST OF SAMUEL: Jonathan will no longer have a drop to drink, nor a fold of purple to cover him. . . . Unhappy Saul, what will the future itself do if the mere pronouncement of it already crushes you?

SAUL: Lord of hosts! My future is in Thy mighty hands. [*He falls unconscious.*]

GHOST OF SAMUEL: Yes, unhappy Saul! You have killed the seers and done away with the interpreters of dreams. Do you think you can kill the future? But now: your future is already on the march, bearing

a sword in its hand. You may kill those who see it, but
you cannot keep it from coming on. It is coming, Saul,
it is upon you; so huge already that you can keep no
one from seeing it.

If you cannot understand me, why did you ask me
to appear? My word, now spoken, will continue to live:
henceforth it will never cease; even if you murdered
the prophets, things themselves would take voice; and
if you refuse to hear it, you yourself will prophesy it.

In three days the Philistines will give battle, and the
chosen of Israel will fall. See! Already the crown is no
longer on your head. God has set it on the head of
David. See, Jonathan himself is putting it there. . . .
Farewell, Saul, your son and you will both soon come
to join me.

[*The* GHOST *vanishes.*]

WITCH [*feebly*]:   I'll be there sooner, Samuel.

[*Silence.*]

SAUL [*as if waking*]:   I am hungry.

WITCH [*kneeling beside* SAUL, *who is still prone*]:   Saul.

SAUL [*raising himself*]:   It is I. . . . I am hungry. . . .
Look, woman; you see that the King needs pity. He is
sick. Give him something to eat. . . .

WITCH: Poor Saul! I have kept this bread; take it.

SAUL [*oblivious*]:   Say: who was speaking here just now?
[*Excited*] Old woman, who is it you were talking to?
Say! What am I doing here? Answer me, quickly:
aren't you the witch of Endor? . . .

WITCH: Poor Saul!

SAUL: The sorceress! No! No! The sorcerers are all dead!
Saul has had them all killed. The witch of Endor is
dead—[*rising*] or going to die.

WITCH [*still kneeling*]:   Ah, you do not need to strike
her, Saul; she will die soon. Leave her alone. . . .

SAUL [*now fully awake, and with growing agitation*]:
Who was it you were speaking to? Wasn't it— Who
told you to call Samuel?

WITCH: Poor Saul!

SAUL: Ah! I will blot out what he said. . . . What he
said must be blotted out of your memory! . . . I
hardly remember now myself.

WITCH: Poor Saul!

SAUL: But—I didn't hear everything. [*Turning furiously
on the* WITCH] Ah, wretched thing, you shall tell me!
. . . I remember now! I fell. . . . What did he say?
What did he say? What did he say?

WITCH: Poor Saul!

SAUL: Ah, tell me, sorceress! Did he name—? Say—
speak—did he name anyone?

WITCH: Have pity!

SAUL: Anyone else—

WITCH: Pity, Saul!

SAUL: But me—

WITCH: Have pity on me.

SAUL: And Jonathan—someone who—

WITCH: No!

SAUL: Come! You do know! Who will succeed me on the
throne?

WITCH: No!

SAUL: You are lying! You are lying! . . . Did he say someone I loved?

WITCH: Saul!

SAUL: Yes? . . . You know it all—David?

WITCH: Why did you name him?

SAUL: No! No! Don't say it! No! No! [*He stabs the* WITCH *with his spear.*]

WITCH: You have wounded me.

SAUL: No! No! Oh no! Look, it was only a little hurt; speak, finish—tell me it was not he.

WITCH [*leaning on her arm,* SAUL *standing over her*]: Saul! You have wounded me mortally. Saul! I was going to die! Why didn't you let me die? Look—my pale blood is dropping on your mantle. . . .

SAUL: No! No! I have done you no harm. Look—speak! Surely you can wait a moment to die. [*Begging*] Ah, answer me.

WITCH: Let my soul—ah, sleep now—it is calm—so quiet.

SAUL: No—not yet.

WITCH: King Saul—

SAUL: What?

WITCH: O King, too easily inclined to open your heart, close the gates.

SAUL: Ah, answer me: did he name—?

WITCH: Let my soul go gently—it is sinking. . . .

SAUL [*taking his head in his hands*]: Ah! . . .

WITCH: King Saul!

68

SAUL [*with a last glimmer of hope*]:   What?

WITCH [*dying*]:   Close your gates! Shut your eyes! Stop
   your ears—and may love's fragrance—

SAUL [*starting*]:   What?

WITCH [*painfully*]:   —no more find the way to your
   heart. All that delights you is your enemy. . . . Free
   yourself! Saul—Saul—

[*She dies.*]

SAUL [*bending closer as her voice fails, as if he still hoped
   for some revelation*]:   What? . . . She is dead. [*He
   looks around him; the fire has gone out; the cave is very
   dark.*] Am I henceforth to struggle alone in darkness?
   [*He gropes, trying to go out.*]

SCENE VIII

---

*The great hall, as in the first act; the curtains on both
sides are closely drawn.* KING SAUL *is seated on the
throne; with robes, crown, and spear.* DAVID, *near by, on
a stool or simply on the floor, is playing his harp before
the* KING.

DAVID: . . . *Around thee pious men give praise*
   The enemies of the King are put to flight.
   The Lord is thy protector, O King.

Here is the new song I have composed for Saul:

. . . *O words filled with goodness, flow, overflow*
    from my heart.
For I must sing, and my song is for the King.   2
May it be like the song of a skillful poet.   [*Pause.*]

Awake, my lute!
Awake, my lute and my harp!
Let my song awaken the dawn. . . .   [*Pause.*]

King Saul! Mount to thy chariot,
Defender of truth, gentleness, and justice!
Mount to thy chariot, King Saul!   [*Pause.*]

All thy warriors await thee . . .
And the Philistines rejoice in their waiting:
Saul sleepeth; Saul cometh not forth!   [*Pause.*]

Mount to thy chariot, valiant King,
Lest the enemies of God should triumph.
Lest they rejoice.   [*Pause.*]

Saul! Saul, awake:
Let my sounding lute go with thee,
Let thy right hand glory in new exploits.   [*Pause.*]

Valiant warrior! Gird on thy sword,
Thy adornments and thy glory.
Yea, thy glory!

SAUL [*somewhat abashed, then yawning, motions for* DAVID *to cease*]: Don't you know something a little lighter?

DAVID: Lighter?

SAUL: Yes. Are you surprised? That's because you don't realize who I am. . . . Come, put your harp away, David. Let's talk. We are here to amuse ourselves. Tell me, how do I look, David?

DAVID: Like a king.

SAUL: No, you don't understand my question. I mean: what do you especially notice about me?

DAVID: Your royalty.

SAUL [*annoyed, then recovering*]: Ah!—even without my beard?

DAVID: You are somewhat less like a king without your beard.

SAUL: It is because you see me better that I seem less a king. Yes. That is why I had my beard removed; I felt less like a king than I looked—whereas now— Tell me that you prefer me this way.

DAVID: I prefer the King.

SAUL: No, David: now I look younger—I am younger. The royal beard made me seem older in your eyes; that is why I didn't like it. . . . It is for you that I had it cut off. . . . David—

[DAVID, *embarrassed, begins playing his harp.* SAUL *is furious, about to strike him.*]

David! [DAVID *starts.*] Don't go away! I was joking.

I wish— Let's talk some more, David. Tell me, do you
pray, sometimes?

DAVID: Yes, King Saul, often.

SAUL: Why? God never answers prayers.

DAVID: What must the King ask for, that he is never
answered? What could a king ask for?

SAUL [*searching for the right answer, then suddenly*]:
What do you ask Him, David?

DAVID [*embarrassed*]:   Never to make me a king.

SAUL [*furious, leaps at* DAVID, *who does not flinch; then
leans over him, lowering his voice*]:   David! David!
Do you want to join with me against God? David, I
could give you—the crown. [*He looks fixedly at* DAVID,
*then, troubled by the latter's sad astonishment and
fright, he decides to burst out laughing.*] Ah! Ha! ha!
Now you see a king with no beard can make a jest!
[*Mounts the throne again, sits; then angrily*] Enough of
this! I do not care to laugh alone. By the Lord, you
took me seriously, I do believe. . . . The crown,
David! So you would like to have the crown! Ah! Ah!
Fie! But what of Jonathan? Do you no longer think of
poor Jonathan? [DAVID *has had enough, starts to leave.*]
Now, now! He wants to leave me again! A wild bird!
So nothing can tame you. . . . Sing, then! Come,
David! Something gay. [DAVID *gestures.*] No! Nothing
gay: you know no light songs! Come, now, do you
never joke, David—not even with your Jonathan?
Never? Then just play. Besides, your singing disturbs
my train of thought. One cannot always be laughing.

[DAVID *begins to play on his harp, and plays to the end of the scene.*]

Ah! Ah! This music flows with my thought. . . . I too was once able to praise God, David. I have sung songs for Him; in His praise my mouth was always open and my tongue inordinately shaken. But now my lips are afraid of speech, they have closed on my secret; and my secret, living within me, cries out with all its strength. [SAUL, *impassioned, begins to speak as in delirium.*] I am exhausted by silence. My mouth is stopped, but my soul is burning; like a vigilant fire, its secret consumes me day and night.

[*Pause; a slight rest in the music.*]

Horror! Horror! Horror! They want to know my secret, and I do not know it myself! It is slowly taking shape in my heart. . . . Music stirs it. . . . Like a bird fluttering against the bars of its cage it rises to my very teeth, leaps toward my lips, leaps and would hurl itself out! . . . David, my soul is in unspeakable torment! Whose name do you hold, my lips? Be tight, O lips of Saul! Draw your royal mantle closer about you, Saul! You are besieged by everything. Stop your ears! Everything is your enemy! Be closed, O gates of my eyes! All that I enjoy is my enemy. Enjoy! O joy! Why am I not a herdsman, to be with him beside the streams? I would look on him the long day through. Oh to be wandering in the burning desert, as long ago, alas, seeking my stray asses; burned in the heat of the air! I would feel no longer the burning in my soul—my

73

soul stirred by your songs—and leaping—from my lips
—toward you—Daoud—my delight.

[DAVID *throws down his harp; it breaks.* SAUL *seems to awaken.*]

Where am I?

David! David! Stay with me. . . .

DAVID: Farewell, Saul! Not for you alone, henceforth, is
your secret unbearable. [*Exit.*]

ACT IV

SCENE I

It is night, but not very dark; a rather narrow stage, showing a garden with a hill rising abruptly; on the left, a running spring surrounded by cypress trees planted at regular intervals.

[JONATHAN, SAKI, THEN DAVID]

JONATHAN: Are you sure this is the place?—Yes, here is the fountain, the cypresses. Saki, how beautiful the night is here! Ah, if I had known of this garden, I should have been coming here often. . . . And now how do you climb up to that plateau?

SAKI: Oh, you have to go a long way around.

JONATHAN: Oh! Oh, that's right—that's right!

SAKI: What is it, Prince? What are you seeking?

JONATHAN: A bird, a small bird; that's why I brought my bow; they tell me that every night it flies over this fountain and lights yonder. Look! Do you see it? Do you see it?

SAKI: No.

JONATHAN: Look! See how it flies! It's circling, circling as if it were going to alight soon.

75

SAKI: But I see nothing at all.

JONATHAN: Look out! There, it's on the ground. Shsh! What? You don't see it? Near that white stone over there! Look: just follow the way my arrow flies. . . . I got it. Run quickly, quickly, and bring back my arrow or the bird.

[*Exit* SAKI. DAVID *emerges from behind a bush.*]

DAVID: Jonathan!

JONATHAN: Ah, David, I thought I should die of anxiety. Tell me quickly! We have only a moment. Saki will be coming back. Why this garden? Wasn't it better to see each other in the palace?

DAVID: No, Jonathan. I must not be seen by anyone. I am leaving. Tonight I must bid you farewell.

JONATHAN: Ah, Daoud—farewell? Can it be true, you are leaving? [*He sits down dully at the edge of the fountain.*]

DAVID: Ah, Jonathan, I haven't the strength to leave you; you must lend me yours too. Do not weaken. Brace up!

JONATHAN: When you are not with me, all pleasure is gone. . . . You are really leaving?

DAVID: I must leave. . . . Saul— [*hesitating*]

JONATHAN: Speak; my father—

DAVID: Can no longer tolerate my presence. He—

JONATHAN: He struck you!

DAVID: Yes—he struck me—struck me. . . . You know his angry moods. Ah, Jonathan, come, stand up. I must see you again, Jonathan.

76

JONATHAN: Where are you going? Without you I have
no strength—

DAVID [*hesitating, then firmly*]:   Where am I going—
now? To the Philistines.

JONATHAN: The Philistines!

DAVID: Quickly, let me explain. Saki will be coming
back; he must not find me here. . . . If your father
found out! . . . But I haven't yet told you the important thing. Listen: the Philistines are again making
ready. Your father is troubled; I don't know what is
wrong, but his mind is not ready for war, and if the
Philistines attack, he is sure to be defeated. The Philistines will attack, that's certain; and that is why I must
put myself at their head. I shall seem to be marching
against you, Jonathan, but if I should take the crown
from Saul, believe me it is only to restore it to you.

JONATHAN [*oblivious*]:   The Philistines! Daoud—you
with the Philistines!

DAVID: Ah, try to understand! Never, if I thought your
father could conquer; but you know he is in the grip
of some anxiety; nothing can distract him—and the
disorder of his soul can be seen in his army. The
soldiers are restless; they will never follow him.

JONATHAN: What of me?

DAVID: You, Jonathan—alas, you would both perish. Ah,
let me go and conquer for you both. But listen, and remember what I am about to tell you. If, on the evening
of the second day, you see the other army camped on
the hilltop overlooking the city—you know, the hill of

77

Gilboa—do not be afraid: this is what you must do.

JONATHAN: Tell me; I will do whatever you say.

DAVID: There, at the end of this garden, hidden among
thorns and lemon trees, you will find the entrance to a
vast cave; I will wait for you there all night. Have no
fear; I do not believe anyone knows the way to it;
come without a light, it might give you away; the sky
is clear and the moon will be full that night. It is not
exactly a cave, but a sort of hollow, partly open above,
so that you can see the sky again after you pass the dark
entrance. I shall be waiting for you, to guide your steps
in the dark. . . . And we shall talk. We shall say how
we must—

[SAKI *is heard singing.*]

JONATHAN: What? Tell me!

DAVID: Saki is coming. Jonathan, my brother! My soul
has sobbed with love. . . . Farewell! Do not forget.
[*Leaving, then turning back*] More than my soul—
ah, Jonathan, more than my soul. [*Exit.*]

JONATHAN: Say no more, David—no more, or you will
take my life away with you.

SAKI: Prince! The bird had flown away; I found nothing
but the arrow.

JONATHAN: Come.

[*Exeunt.*]

SCENE II

———————————————

A desert. A level waste of sand rising vaguely in dunes. Burning sun. On the left, lying on a dune, the DEMON, *wearing an enormous brown cloak, which drags behind him over the sand.*

[S A U L ; A B L A C K D E M O N]

SAUL [*enters right, bareheaded, a gnarled stick in his hand; he is without his royal robes, wearing only undergarments*]:   Take care! the wit of kings may evaporate in such a sun. Now, what was it I came looking for? . . . Ah, my asses . . . every trace disappears like water in the sand. [*He leans down; then, starting up*] Brrr! A snake.

DEMON [*without moving*]:   Won't harm you.

SAUL [*not very surprised*]:   What?

DEMON: I say he won't harm you, not you. . . . Come on! You're not going to be afraid of snakes at your age, old monarch!

SAUL: This little beggar has no respect for me. [*Threatens to beat him.*]

DEMON: I must say, King Saul, that you are not so respectable any more without your beard. [*The* KING *strikes him, prods him with his stick.*] Ah, no! No! Don't tickle me; I might laugh too much. [*Both writhe with*

79

laughter.] King Saul, where did you leave your crown? With David?

SAUL [*putting his hand to his head*]:   I have been skipping a bit through the desert. Maybe it fell off.

DEMON: Beware of the desert sun; you haven't enough hair any more to go without your crown. Take my hat. [*He hands him his cap; the* KING *puts it on.*] King Saul, where did you leave your cloak? Your fine purple cloak, King Saul? With David?

SAUL: I was too hot. . . . It's very hot in the desert.

DEMON: Yes, but at night it's very cold in the desert. Take my cape.

SAUL: What will you wear?

DEMON: I am used to the desert.

SAUL [*stripping him*]:   Well! You hadn't told me how handsome you are.

DEMON [*naked*]:   Oh! A little dark perhaps. . . .

SAUL: Oh no, not at all.

DEMON: It's a matter of taste. [SAUL *puts on the enormous cloak, which drags behind him.*] And say, where did you leave your scepter?

SAUL [*mechanically*]:   With David. It was too heavy. This stick is more useful in the desert.

DEMON [*holding out his hand*]:   Let me see it. Why, King Saul! It's a serpent.

SAUL: You little rascal! [*He laughs.*] A serpent! A serpent! Here, now! None of your pranks! [*The stick turns into a serpent and runs away.*] Run and get it, now.

[*The* KING *gets down on all fours.*]

DEMON [*standing quite erect on the hillock*]:   I must say
you don't look too much like a king, that way. [*He
laughs; SAUL stands up.*] Do you know how I recognized you, Saul? By your beauty.

SAUL [*looking proud in his fool's cloak, but anxious*]:
Ah! Really? Do I still look—

DEMON: How long it has been since I saw you! Young
Saul came here once, do you remember? He was looking for his stray asses.

SAUL [*sighing*]:   Ah! My asses!

DEMON: King Saul! Where did you leave your asses?

SAUL: Do you know where? Tell me, do you know?

DEMON [*pulling SAUL's coattail*]:   Come on, won't you?
We'll look for them together. [*They go behind the
dune, and are overheard*] Oh, say, King Saul! I am
tired; carry me.

SAUL [*tenderly*]:   Nice boy! Sweet boy! . . .

SCENE III

_____

*The throne room of the palace, as in the first act. People
are crowding in to see, but leave free passage, right, from
entrance to throne, for the KING to enter. Apart, right, the
BARBER and JOEL observe the crowd and talk in a low
voice. Most have their backs to the audience.*

[THE CROWD, THEN SAUL AND JONATHAN]

FIRST MAN: What then?

SECOND MAN: Then they brought him back to the palace.

FIRST MAN: Was he still singing?

SECOND MAN: I should say he was singing—and dancing too! They couldn't hold him.

THIRD MAN: The Prince wanted them to put his clothes and his crown on him, but he was jumping about so the crown wouldn't stay on his head.

[*They laugh.*]

FOURTH MAN: And yet it's a shame! For once we were given the chance to choose a king, and we chose—

FIFTH MAN: David chose himself.

THIRD MAN: But they say he doesn't want to be king?

FIFTH MAN: Don't believe that! Who doesn't want to be king?

SECOND MAN: Would you like to be?

FIRST MAN: Well, what would you do if you were king, eh?

FIFTH MAN: The first thing, I would boot David out.

[*They laugh.*]

SIXTH MAN [*approaching angrily*]:   Who is abusing David?

THIRD, FOURTH, AND FIFTH MEN: No one is abusing David.

SIXTH MAN: Just wait until he comes back, and you will see whether he gets booted out—or Saul.

82

SEVERAL VOICES [*not in affirmation, rather in indifference*]:
Oh, Saul! . . . Saul! . . .

AN OLD JEW [*who has been listening, to the* SECOND MAN]:
And what was Saul saying?

SECOND MAN: How should we know? He was just shouting.

THIRD MAN: He himself doesn't know what he is saying.

OLD JEW: We should always listen to prophets.

FOURTH AND FIFTH MEN: But Saul is no prophet.

[*The crowd is still growing.*]

SEVENTH MAN: Yes, he is! Saul is a prophet; I was there
when he danced before Samuel.

EIGHTH MAN: Is it true that before he died Samuel gave
David his blessing?

A CHILD: Is it true that King Saul has had his beard cut
off?

[*All laugh; the crowd spreads; conversation moves from
place to place.*]

NINTH, SECOND, AND THIRD MEN: Yes, it's true.

FIRST MAN AND OTHERS: What a farce! Has anyone seen
him? Really! His whole beard?

TENTH MAN: I don't think that's right, a king with no
beard.

FOURTH MAN: But David hasn't got a beard.

TENTH MAN: He has no beard yet. . . .

FIFTH MAN: Besides, David is handsome.

FOURTH MAN [*to the* TENTH]:   What about Jonathan?

SEVERAL VOICES: Oh, Jonathan! When will he ever have
one!

83

[*A stir on the right.*]

OTHERS: Shsh! Shsh! It's the King.

A MAN [*very loud*]:   Why shsh?

WHISPERS: It's true! It's true, his beard is gone!

FIRST MAN [*to a group*]:   Don't shout like that!

ONE OF THE GROUP [*turning to the* FIRST]:   Oh, he doesn't
  hear a thing you say to him, not since the other day.

FIFTH MAN OR ANOTHER: It's true, he looks sick!

SIXTH MAN: Jonathan too!

FIFTH MAN AND OTHERS: Oh, him! . . .

A MAN IN FRONT [*away from the audience*]:   Hey, stop
  pushing!

A CHILD: Jacob! Jacob! Lift me up. I want to see the
  King without his beard.

[*All laugh. A stir indicates* SAUL's *approach; the crowd
divides sharply on both sides of the throne. All during this
part of the scene it is apparent that the* KING *is coming;
the crowd sees him, but he is still hidden from the audience.*]

FIRST MAN: Why is he coming in alone like this? I
  thought he had guards with him.

THIRD MAN: Oh, no one listens to him any more: when
  he calls, people go the other way.

[SAUL *enters, hesitantly, like a drunken man or, better
still, like someone surrounded by a mocking and hostile
crowd; his eyes look mad, now disdainful, now anxious;
he is leaning on* JONATHAN, *who is himself faint and
whose sad and shameful eyes look imploringly at the peo-*

ple. SAUL *brandishes his spear ridiculously; the crowd stirs; some stand back.*]

THIRD MAN: There's no need to be afraid: his spear has no head on it.

FIRST MAN: It's true they won't let him have weapons any more?

SECOND MAN: They are pretty well right, there!

FIFTH MAN: It seems he tried to kill David. . . .

[*One sees that* JONATHAN *is suffering horribly from all these remarks; someone in the crowd hurls an overripe fruit, which splashes on* SAUL'S *back.*]

SOMEONE [*with hatred*]:   Take that!

[*Several others turn around with indignation; commotion and uproar. The* KING *mounts to the throne; beside him,* JONATHAN, *with head in his hands.* SAUL *gestures as if he would speak.*]

CRIES: Silence! Silence!

SAUL [*standing*]:   Dear Hebrews!

[*Many writhe with laughter.*]

OTHERS: What did he say? What did he say?

SAUL: Dear Hebrew people! [*More writhing and laughter. The* KING'S *anxiety is evident; he speaks slowly and with difficulty, fumbling for words.*] On the eve of an important battle . . .

[*His voice is drowned by a growing commotion, left; the crowd moves left, where someone is being questioned. Attention shifts to the newcomers; in the growing tumult the* KING'S *voice is lost, and these words are heard:*]

85

Yes, on Mount Gilboa . . .

OTHERS: What? What?

THE FIRST: David's army—yes, the Philistines. You can see them from the square. . . .

OTHERS: Where? Say, where?

[*At this moment a powerful voice rises above all others and calls out solemnly:*]

King Saul! The army of David has camped on Mount Gilboa!

ALL: Let's go and see! Let's go!

[*Uproar, stampede.*]

LITTLE GIRLS: Hurry! Quick!

JONATHAN [*raising his head, until now hidden in his hands; he seems to be coming out of a dream; looks about him; looks at* SAUL, *is heard to say*]:   The evening of the second day. Ah, David! David! [*Exit, transported with joy or anxiety, in the opposite direction from the crowd.*]

SAUL [*angry and shouting like a schoolmaster after his pupils*]:   Will you stay! Will you please—when I am speaking—now, will you—

[*Starts to run after them; then awkwardly throws his spear; then goes piteously and picks it up. The stage is now empty. On the steps of the throne a child is sobbing:* SAKI. *The* KING *comes back.*]

SCENE IV

――――――――――――

[THE KING, SAKI]

SAUL: Saki! Is it you, boy? [*Very tenderly*] Are you
weeping for me? Poor Saki. [SAKI *still weeping; the*
KING, *embarrassed, stopping between phrases*] You
mustn't pity me. . . . Is it because you love me?

SAKI [*sobbing*]: They have all left you—all left you. . . .

SAUL: And that is why you are weeping! Poor little
Saki. . . . But that doesn't matter, you know. (Oh, I
wish I could console this child!) So you love me, Saki,
a little?

SAKI: Oh, very much! Very much!

SAUL: Well! And why?

SAKI: You are good to me.

SAUL: Me! Good?

SAKI: Yes; on the terrace you used to let me drink from
your—

SAUL [*disgusted with himself*]: Ah! Wine.

SAKI: And then—and then—

SAUL: What?

SAKI: You are alone.

SAUL [*gradually stirred by a new emotion*]: Why no,
you see I am not alone, dear Saki: you are with me. Ah,
I didn't know anyone could grieve for me. What should
I do?

[*Enter several officers led by the* HIGH PRIEST, *who is dumbfounded.*]

HIGH PRIEST [*as if he had something very important to say*]:   King Saul—

SAUL [*interrupting him*]:   Wait awhile! You see that I am talking—

[*Exeunt, with despairing gestures, all but* SAUL *and* SAKI.]

SAUL [*playfully*]:   Would you think it fun to be king, Saki?

SAKI: Oh, no!

SAUL: What! You wouldn't want to be the king?

SAKI: I don't know.

SAUL: "I don't know." Look here, do you want to try on my crown? [SAUL *takes it, about to put it on* SAKI's *head.*]

SAKI [*pushing it away*]:   No.

SAUL [*letting up for a moment*]:   Tell me, Saki, why didn't you follow David?

SAKI: I don't know.

SAUL [*more and more annoyed*]:   "I don't know." Don't you love David?

SAKI: Oh, yes; but—

SAUL: But?

SAKI: I would rather stay with you.

SAUL: But, Saki, I thought you were leaving me for Jonathan. In the evening, lately, on the terrace, you would leave me—

SAKI: For Jonathan, yes.

88

SAUL: Well! David and Jonathan—are together, aren't they?

SAKI: Often, yes.

SAUL: And they are more fun than an old king.

SAKI: Oh, you are not old, King Saul.

SAUL [*holding his crown on his knees, lifts it from time time as if to put it on* SAKI's *head; but withdraws each time as* SAKI, *sitting at his feet, raises his head*]: You think so? You think I still know how to joke?

SAKI: David and Jonathan don't joke.

SAUL: Ah! And what do they do?

SAKI: Nothing.

SAUL: What do they say?

SAKI: Nothing.

SAUL: They talk, don't they?

SAKI: Yes.

SAUL: Well, what do they say?

SAKI: I don't know. [*As he lowers his head, in a kind of embarrassment,* SAUL *suddenly forces the crown on his head. It comes down over his eyes.*]

SAUL [*with forced pleasantry*] Ah! You don't know! Whang! The crown!

SAKI [*frightened*]: Oh! What's that?

SAUL: It's the crown.

SAKI: It's over my eyes—I can't see!

SAUL [*bursting with laughter*]: "I can't see!" Ah! Ha ha ha!

SAKI: It hurts. . . . Oh, take it off, King Saul!

89

SAUL [*holding the crown, pressing it down with both hands*]: What does David say?

SAKI [*sobbing*]: Nothing, I tell you! Oh, take it off!

SAUL [*slapping* SAKI's *hands, as* SAKI *struggles*]: Leave it! Leave it alone! . . . It's just for fun. And what does Jonathan say?

SAKI: Nothing—King Saul. I swear.

SAUL: "Nothing, nothing." Just tell me what?

SAKI: He calls him Daoud.

SAUL: I knew that—what else?

SAKI [*desperate*]: Nothing! Nothing! Nothing, King Saul! [SAUL, *tragically, takes the crown.* SAKI, *putting his hand to his forehead*] See, I am bleeding.

SAUL [*almost triumphantly*]: Ah! Now you see that I am not good! [*Then, suddenly, bending over him with great tenderness*] Did I hurt you, Saki? [SAKI, *still frightened, slips away from* SAUL, *going out slowly, backwards.*] And what did they say when they caught me? That I was crazy? Eh? [*Confidentially*] Tell me, did you know that I ran away? Eh? Now they won't let me go out any more without my crown. . . . Jonathan wants— [*Perceiving only now that* SAKI *is trying to get away; just as the latter looks back for the last time*] Oh, Saki, you are leaving me [*very sadly*], you said you loved me, Saki? [SAKI *is touched, comes back to the* KING, *who leans over, confidentially.*] Listen: my stray asses! You know about my asses. Well, I know where they are! Let's go together and look for them! Do you want to? [*Going*] We'll go away! We'll run away!

SCENE V

———————————

*A cave, or rather an open den; on the left the vaulted top
has fallen in, allowing the light of the full moon to shine
through brush and hanging vines: large rocks on the left;
on the right, under the vault of the cave, it is very dark;
a sloping path leads into this part from the back. Enter*
SAUL, *coming down, feeling his way with his feet.*

SAUL: Well! A spring. . . . It's slippery. I almost fell.
The ground is wet. Where are you taking me?

DEMON: [*Silent.*]

SAUL: Here? . . . Come, come, answer me. You keep
on, the same way. You mustn't think you can lead me
wherever you wish, and not find what I am looking for.

[*Moving left*] Well! This is a rather curious place!
Not a bad spot for a talk. . . . After all, you know, I
don't need so much as all this to find those asses. . . .
Only, at my age, you are making me walk too far! I get
tired, you know. [*Looking for a place to sit, comes
back to the right; sits on a sort of natural seat, in the
dark of the cave.*] You sit there [*pointing vaguely to a
place opposite him. The* DEMON *is about to sit.*] No,
don't sit on the ground: it's damp. [*Handing him the
crown*] Sit on this. [*The* DEMON *sits on the crown.*]
First, you must tell me— [*Sneezes, indicating he is
taking cold.*] If we're not looking for my asses, why did
you bring me here? [*Sneezes.*]

DEMON: Bless you!

SAUL: Tell me.

DEMON: Hee! Hee! Hee!

SAUL: Ah, I don't like people to laugh when I am not joking.

DEMON: Hee! It's so funny, King Saul! You know who it is you are going to see?

SAUL: Ah, Saki, I don't feel a bit like joking now! But tell me, who is it we are going to see? [*Rises, goes toward the* DEMON.]

DEMON: Sh! Sh! Just listen.

[*The sound of steps and voices approaching from the left.*]

SAUL: Ah! Jonathan!

DEMON: And who else?

SAUL [*murmuring*]:   David!

DEMON: Say thank you!

DAVID [*with* JONATHAN; *they are lighted by the moon*]:
. . . Three times! I will have the trumpets sounded three times. When you hear the first, get ready. It will be a little before dawn. . . . Persuade Saul. After the third, I can no longer be responsible. You must both take refuge here before day.

SAUL [*starts toward them; the* DEMON *pulls him back by his cloak*]: Oh! He is counseling treason!

DEMON: If they see you, they will run away.

JONATHAN: Farewell, David.

DAVID [*his forehead on* JONATHAN's *shoulder*]: Ah, Jonathan!

92

DEMON [*pulling* SAUL *back*]:   Here! Come back! Let's lie down. Let them come nearer. Pretend to be asleep. You will see better.

[SAUL *lies where he was sitting. The* DEMON *disappears.*]

DAVID [*lifting his head*]:   Farewell. Go now. Leave me alone for a while. I need to pray.

JONATHAN: What do you ask of God?

DAVID: Don't you know, Jonathan? Ah, to take this crown from my path.

SAUL [*aside, bantering*]:   How simple that is!

DEMON: Shsh!

JONATHAN: Farewell.

[DAVID *kneels among the rocks, almost turning his back to the audience.* JONATHAN *moves to the right, sees* SAUL, *and returns hurriedly to* DAVID.]

David! David! It's my father. [DAVID, *absorbed in his prayer, does not move.* JONATHAN, *desperately:*] My father is here, David.

DAVID [*still praying*]:   I have not finished my prayer. Leave me!

JONATHAN [*turns away again, looks at* SAUL. *To* DAVID]:   He is asleep.

[*During this scene the moonlight has been slowly moving to the right; it now touches* SAUL's *crown, lying on the ground.*]

Ah! His crown has fallen to the ground. . . .

DAVID: I haven't finished praying yet. Be quiet!

[*Silent stillness.*]

SAUL: Isn't he coming nearer?

[DAVID *rises.*]

JONATHAN: What are you going to do?

DAVID: You will see. [*Takes up the crown, sets it beside* SAUL's *forehead.*] Tell him, Jonathan. You must make him believe.

SAUL [*aside*]:   I am trembling so, he will know . . .

JONATHAN: He won't believe me.

DAVID [*with a sudden idea*]:   Ah! [*He draws his sword, cuts a large piece from the royal cloak, takes it away with him.*] Let him know I did it; that instead of this piece of his cloak I could have taken his life. But look! He is waking! Come, quickly, let's go!

[*Exeunt, left.*]

SAUL [*rises and goes into the moonlight, looks at himself; almost indecently clothed, in his slashed cloak; then laughing derisively*]:   They are too good to me!

94

ACT V

It is night. The scene is a vague mountainous place, very indistinct. Somewhere on the right, Saul's tent.

SCENE I

[JOEL AND THE BARBER, *before the tent*]

BARBER: No orders yet?

JOEL: Orders? Oh, orders, yes, lots of orders, but no direction.

BARBER: Is it true the Hebrews are divided?

JOEL: Divided? Not at all; they are all for David.

BARBER: The devil you say! This promises to be a curious battle! [*Sneering*] What about Saul? Is he for David too?

JOEL [*turning serious*]:   Hold your tongue, barber; Saul is a tottering old man. And this war is no more than a sham battle; his defeat is already accomplished in his heart.

BARBER: Then, what will you do, Joel?

JOEL: What will you do, barber? Are you asking me for

95

advice? Since when have I made it my business to
guide your thinking? Make way: here is Saul.

[*Enter* SAUL *and* JONATHAN. *Torches light the inside of
the tent.*]

SCENE II

––––––––––––––

[SAUL, JONATHAN, OTHERS, WITH SAKI]

SAUL [*to* JONATHAN]:   You see how my hands are trembling!

JONATHAN: Poor Father!

SAUL: What do you think would do me most good? To
  drink some wine? Or not to drink? I think it would be
  better to drink. . . . Go, Saki. [*Exit* SAKI.] Today I
  couldn't kill, even an enemy—I haven't the strength
  within me. It is time I should come nearer to God . . .
  [*In a louder voice*] Now leave me. Night will soon be
  over, and I need to be alone, to meditate. [*A stir.*] You,
  Jonathan, stay with me; I want to speak further with
  you.

[*Exeunt others.* SAUL *strides back and forth in silence.*]

JONATHAN: Father, I have but a very few minutes.

SAUL [*sneezing*]:   Let down that curtain. [*Sneezing*] I
  caught cold the other day in a cave. In fact, you probably know the cave; it is not far from here. And that
  prowler, David, certainly knows it.

96

JONATHAN [*more and more impatient with* SAUL's *insist-ence*]: But please, Father, let's hurry. This night is all that stands between us and the battle; we should either be getting ready or asleep.

SAUL [*pithily*]: We must be getting ready, my son. To-night my whole soul is getting ready.

JONATHAN: I mean, ready for action, Father. What are you trying to tell me?

SAUL: Ah, precisely that, Jonathan. When I was a man of action, I did not understand. There is a time to act, and a time to repent of one's acts. My son, you must understand that there are things more important to the soul than the victories of an army. . . .

JONATHAN: But, Father, when were you ever a man of action?

SAUL: I know, I know; I have been more a man of de-sires. But for that too, my child, the time has come when I would repent.

[JONATHAN, *more and more distressed, makes ready to leave.*]

What! You are going?

JONATHAN: But time is flying! I have everything to see to. . . . I'll come back in a moment, Father.

SAUL: Jonathan! Jonathan! When my heart trembles, you leave me! Can't you stay and talk with me a mo-ment? . . . My son, I am a tenderer father than I was, believe me.

JONATHAN: Alas! . . . Here is Saki . . . Father, let me go.

97

SAUL [*to* JONATHAN *and* SAKI]:   Ah, leave me, both of
you! I am a fool to seek support in you! . . . Saki, take
this wine away. It is better for me not to drink. Get out.
Get out.

[*Exit* JONATHAN. SAKI *remains, unnoticed, in a corner of
the tent.*]

JONATHAN [*going*]:   Father, when I come back, will you
follow me?

SAUL: Perhaps. [*Calling him back*] One moment, Jonathan! Jonathan, don't be sad. Come back in a short
while: I will follow you. . . . But let me pray a little
now.

SCENE III

———————

[SAUL, SAKI, *at first unnoticed;*
THE DEMON *outside*]

SAUL [*thinking he is alone*]:   Ah! Ah! Let me collect myself. What am I?

DEMON [*hidden outside*]:   Saul!

SAUL [*going to the door*]:   Jonathan? [*He looks.*] No, I
am alone. [*Kneeling*] My God, what am I before thee—

DEMON [*hidden*]:   Saul!

SAUL: —that Thou shouldst overwhelm me with desire?
When I seek support in anything, it gives way. There
is no strength or stay in me. [*Distracted*] What I love
in him, above all, is his strength. The movement of his

98

loins is beautiful! I saw him coming down from the
mountain; he seems always ready to leap. . . . [*Haggard*] Enough, my lips. [*He rises.*]

DEMON [*plaintively*]:   Saul!

SAUL: I am distracted.

DEMON: Saul!

SAUL: Hmmm! Someone is calling me. [*He goes to the
door of the tent.*]

SAKI: Don't open it, King Saul!

SAUL: What! It's you, Saki! What are you doing here?

SAKI: I am afraid for you.

SAUL: Were you calling me?

SAKI: No.

SAUL: Ah, it's someone outside.

SAKI: No! Do not open the door. . . . There is everything out there; the night is full!

DEMON: Saul!

SAKI: Don't let him in. . . .

SAUL: Oh, little closed heart, don't you hear? Someone
is calling me. [SAUL *goes out with a torch.*]

DEMON [*still very plaintive*]:   Saul!

SAUL [*approaches, stooping*]:   Poor little fellow! He's
trembling! Is it the cold? [*Touching him*] Why, he's
frozen, the poor child! Come! We'll be warmer in my
tent. Come along; I will get you warm. [*The* DEMON
does not budge.] Oh, I can't carry you, little fellow!
[*Lifting him*] How terribly heavy he is! [*Carrying
him.*]

[*Exit* SAKI.]

Saki is going. Good riddance! He's leaving the wine. I'll give you a drink. [*Putting him down*] Oof! Here, snuggle up in my cloak. [*Sits.*]

DEMON [*wrapping himself in the cloak*]:   It's torn.

SAUL [*smiling*]:   Yes, David cut a piece out of this side.

DEMON [*chuckling*]:   Ah! Ha ha!

SAUL: What?

DEMON: Nothing.

SAUL: Is that funny?

DEMON: Yes.—I'm thirsty.

SAUL [*handing him the jug*]:   Drink some.—Is that better?—There, close to me.—Now be quiet; I have a lot of thinking to do.

JONATHAN [*outside*]:   Father!

SAUL [*ashamed*]:   Good! Jonathan! . . . Don't come in. [*To the* DEMON] Hide yourself.

JONATHAN: Father, come with me. Come now; it is time.

SAUL [*very embarrassed*]:   I am coming—just a moment. . . . Go ahead, I will follow you.

[*The* DEMON *appears, looks at* JONATHAN *and sniggers.*]

JONATHAN: Oh, what is that?

SAUL: It's a child who was shivering with cold—I took him into my tent.

JONATHAN [*profoundly sad*]:   Ah?

SAUL [*ashamed*]:   Yes.

JONATHAN [*increasingly desperate*]:   Father, let him go now! Come!

SAUL [*not moving, foolishly*]:   Yes.

JONATHAN: Oh, Father! Father, don't you love me more than that child—a little more?

SAUL [*almost sobbing*]:   Hush, Jonathan! . . . Jonathan! I beg you! You don't know how hard it is!

JONATHAN: Hard to do what? Poor Father—how tormented you are!

SAUL: Jonathan—you are too young to understand me: I feel that I am becoming quite strange! My value is in my complexity. Listen, I want to tell you a few secrets: you think I was asleep the other night—in the cave.

JONATHAN [*pretending not to understand*]:   The cave?

SAUL: Yes—you know—when David—

JONATHAN: David?

SAUL [*angry*]:   Yes, David—and you—were planning my defeat—and he cut off a piece of my cloak, to teach you better to betray me. Ah! Ah! The understanding between you two is perfect. . . . Both so mindful of me! You can thank him for me! You can thank him, I say, Jonathan! [*The* DEMON *chuckles.*] Yes indeed, give him my thanks. He thinks I am finished!

[*A call of trumpets is heard.*]

JONATHAN: Ah!

SAUL: Ah!—the signal!

JONATHAN: Come, Father, come. Ah, out of pity for yourself!

SAUL: You are weeping! Jonathan! Jonathan, my son— you understand at least, don't you, how it hurts me— how it hurts me to make you weep? But listen to this

101

proverb, one of mine. [*Escorting him to the threshold
of the tent, pompously*] With what shall man console
himself for a fall, if not with what made him fall? [*Dis-
missing him*] Go now, leave me—quickly! . . . To the
cave! Run! I will join you in a moment.

[*Groups of soldiers are heard, partly seen, passing. Exit*
JONATHAN.]

SCENE IV

[SAUL, THE DEMON]

SAUL [*forgetting the* DEMON]:   Ah, what am I waiting for
now? Why do I not get up and act? My will! My will!
I call to it now like a shipwrecked sailor hailing a ship
he sees disappearing in the distance—going—going.
. . . I strengthen everything against me. [*Sees the* DE-
MON *drinking.*] Here, leave me now. Good-by. . . . Go
along. I need to rest.

[*The* DEMON *does not budge.*]

DEMON: You will never rest again, King Saul.

SAUL: I will never rest again? Oh, why do you tell me
that, child?

DEMON: Because I will never leave you, King Saul.

SAUL: Never!

DEMON: Never again.

SAUL: You will never leave me. But why?

DEMON: Because you took care of me.

SAUL: Care! What did I do, you little scoundrel? I only
wrapped you in part of my cloak—you were shivering
with cold!

DEMON: Yes. But now I have got fearfully warm. Just
touch me. Feel how my skin is burning!

SAUL: No! Stop. . . . I don't want to. Go away. I beg
you, take pity on me; I took pity on you.

DEMON: Pity! Oh, come now, Saul! Don't tell me it
wasn't for your own pleasure that you brought me in—
eh?—to have me in the fold of your cloak? Eh? Saul!
Saul! Come on, now, Saul, amuse me a little—we are
sad. Tell me, have I done you any harm? Why are you
angry with me?

SAUL [*trying to break off*]:   I want to pray.

DEMON [*heedless*]:   And then, you know—if you want
to have pity—I am not alone; there are lots of others,
out there.

SAUL [*tempted, despite himself*]:   Ah! Others? Where?

DEMON: Right there, outside the door.

[SAUL *goes and lifts the tent flap. Enter* DEMONS, *jostling
one another.*]

SCENE V

[SAUL AND THE DEMONS]

SAUL: Oh, there are so many! Come along! Come in! If
I refused my lodging to a single one, I should be afraid

it might be the most attractive—or maybe the most wretched.

[*The tent flap falls. A vague, continuous hum now fills the tent. The* DEMONS *stir in a swarm.*]

FIRST DEMON [*to the others*]:   The King said something so funny awhile ago!

[*Confusion. Whispers to the others; they all laugh. A second trumpet is heard.*]

SAUL: Ah! Ah! The night is nearly over. We must hurry!

[*Enter* JONATHAN.]

JONATHAN [*outside*]:   Father!

SAUL [*leaping to the tent door, stretching his cloak over it to conceal the scene inside*]:   Don't come in!

JONATHAN [*grieved*]:   Ah! Come!

SAUL [*urgently*]:   For the love of the God of David, fly, Jonathan! Run quickly! I will follow you.

[*Exit* JONATHAN. *The stage is filling with a tumult of soldiers. Noise off stage—uproar of demons in the tent. Day is gradually coming. But inside the tent it remains dark, lighted only by torches.* SAUL *advances to the footlights, facing the audience, his voice rising above the noise.*]

Before I go, I should like to sum up in a few words. [*Noise of* DEMONS *increases.*] Be quiet, you roisterers! You surely see that I am speaking to the audience! [*To the audience*] With what shall man console himself—

DEMONS: But you've already said that—you've already said it. . . . Ah! Ha ha!

[*Uproar. The increasing racket of the* DEMONS *is produced by steady music.*]

SAUL [*turning to the* DEMONS]:   Well then, come on! If you want to steal the play, at least put on a performance, show us what you can do.

[*The* DEMONS *roll and tumble. A regulated uproar.* SAUL *looks on, long and gravely. Then, in disgust*]

This is not very pretty.

DEMONS: But, Saul, you haven't taught us anything.

SAUL: Enough, now! Enough! [*He is jostled, falls to his knees; then, taking advantage of the situation*] I want to pray.

[*Noise off stage.* SAUL *backs toward the door, on his knees; the jostling of the* DEMONS *is gradually getting the best of him.*]

[*Praying*] Is there no remedy for my desire, other than to satisfy it? [*Backing still farther*] Let me sum up. Let me sum up! [*Haggard*] Ah, little fellows, you leave me no more room. [*In a lower voice*] I am completely cut off.

[*Day breaks. A third trumpet call is heard.* SAUL, *half rising, snatches open the tent flap. The* DEMONS *vanish in a flood of daylight. The music has stopped.*]

SCENE VI

———————————

[VARIOUS]

SAUL [*a loud voice, in the silence*]:   It is too late! Day is here. [*Comes out of the tent, toward the left, kneels or*

half sits on the ground, his hands in the grass.] Ah, how
refreshing the cool air is. . . . This is the hour when
the herdsmen are bringing their flocks from the stables.
The grass is bathed in dew. . . .

[JOEL *has entered, with other soldiers of David's army.*]

JOEL [*seeing* SAUL]:   Well! He's praying. . . .

SAUL [*engrossed, not seeing them*]:   I am tempted.

SOLDIER [*to the others*]:   Men of David, make haste and
notify the King that Saul is here—without arms. Run!
David does not want him to be killed.

[*Exeunt.* JOEL *remains.*]

SAUL [*still engrossed*]:   . . . Bathed in dew. . . .

[JOEL *approaches the* KING, *then suddenly rises up behind him, with his hand lifted.*]

Oh! Oh! Oh! This is a most cowardly temptation; it
assails me from behind.

[JOEL *strikes him,* SAUL *falls.* JOEL *snatches his crown,
carries it to* DAVID, *who arrives with a numerous escort.
At a command from* DAVID, JOEL *is seized. A stir. It is now
full daylight.*]

DAVID: Oh, evil day! Here! Take this man away. Kill him
and give his corpse to the beasts of the field. Shame on
him who lifts his hand against the elect of the Lord!
This crown, with all its weight, has now fallen on my
head. [*He bends down to* SAUL, *takes up the crown,
which at first he had caused to be laid beside* SAUL,
and puts it on his own head. Bowing very low] I did not
detest you, King Saul. [*Rising*] Jonathan too, you say?
Oh unhappy day! Let him be brought here. Let him

be laid beside Saul, let them be joined in death. What are those cries and lamentations out there? My soul is filled with grief.

[*A cortège brings the body of* JONATHAN.]

O mountains of Gilboa, let there be no dew and no honey upon you! [*Bending over* JONATHAN] I did my best, Jonathan! I did my best, Jonathan, my brother! [*Rising*] Come, now, let us rise! Let the bodies of Saul and the Prince be brought to the palace; let them be laid on a royal litter. Let the people form a procession, and accompany my grief with their sobs and their lamentations. Musicians! Let funeral music sound.

[*Exeunt in full procession, to the sound of a funeral march.*]

END

Bathsheba

1912

TO MME LUCIE DELARUE-MARDRUS

CHARACTERS

DAVID

JOAB

A SERVANT

SCENE I

[DAVID, KING OF JUDAH;
JOAB, CAPTAIN OF DAVID'S ARMY]

KING DAVID, *wearing half-priestly, half-warlike garb, is
on his knees reciting a prayer which he is just transcrib-
ing.*

DAVID: ". . . Even the strong man faileth, the young
man faltereth,
But he that putteth his trust in God—"
[*Enter* JOAB.]
You have come in too soon, Joab; I have not finished
my prayer.
Be quiet. Where was I? . . . Ah!—
"Shall not falter.
God will lend His strength to him that is weary;
He shall have wings like the eagles."
I first wrote: "Their wings shall grow . . ."
But: "He shall have wings like the eagles" is better.
What do you want with me?
JOAB: The Hittite has returned.
DAVID: What Hittite? Where has he returned from?
JOAB: From the siege of Rabbah; he brings news.
He is merely a simple soldier
Whom the King—

DAVID: Bah! Are you jealous of him, Joab?

Uriah the Hittite is the most valiant of my men.

I feigned ignorance, just to hear you lie.

Shall I forget who triumphed over the Philistines at
    Gath?

Who defended the fields of Pas-dammim?

Tell me: who struck down the two lions of Moab? He
    did.

And the four giant sons of Rapha? He did.

JOAB: Perhaps—

DAVID: Just listen: At harvest time

In the cave of Adullam, I longed in vain for cool water;

The Philistines were encamped in the valley;

For two days they had occupied Bethlehem.

You know the bitter well at Bethlehem;

That day I thirsted for its water,

I longed after it. . . .

Who broke through the camp of the enemy?

Who put his life in jeopardy to bring me a cup of that
    water?

Who was it? Tell me.

It was the Hittite, Uriah.

It's vain, Joab, for you to pretend to forget these things;

At the very brink of the grave I should recall them still.

I do not want it said that anyone

Has obliged the King without profit.

I intend that Uriah shall eat at my table;

All I possess is his.

I expect him at the palace; send him that word.

[JOAB *motions to a servant, transmits the King's order.*]

   He is the friend of Nathan, isn't he?

JOAB: Yes, Sire, Nathan the prophet.

[JOAB *makes as if to leave.*]

DAVID: Don't go away.

[*The King is silent for a few moments.*]

   I fear the prophet Nathan. Why do you smile?

   It's because you do not know his power;

   The people obey his voice;

   Even I am like a child before him and keep still;

   When he says: "The Lord—" he sounds like God Him-
      self.

   To be sure, I have heard tell of other prophets;

   They prophesy and then they are silent;

   But this man's voice keeps on.

   I must force him to silence.

   Dear Joab, I am afraid of Nathan.

   There comes an hour in the day when the might of
      kings diminishes;

   There comes a day in life when a man who has walked
      long feels weary.

   I remember the virtues, the prayers of my youth;

   Then it was I who conversed with God.

   I remember King Saul. . . . Now, like him,

   I see the shadow lengthening before my steps.

   The Lord no longer listens to me;

   No longer speaks through my mouth,

   No longer speaks to me. . . .

But lately I can hardly bear His silence.
I will force Him to speak.

As a starving dog gnaws a bone that has no more meat,
Or as a mother presses her dead child in her arms,
All night I have pressed the name of my God to my
     lips:
Between my hands joined in prayer
I have warmed all that remained of my faith in prayer;
And lo, the sound of a wing above me. . . .
It was the hour when the lamp's flame falters,
When the oil of the lamp gives out,
The hour when the valiant man takes fright,
When virtuous resolve gives way,
When kings and men are drugged with the wine of
     sleep. . . .
And yet my soul remained vigilant;
I waited upon God all night.
—And lo, like a breath above me
The airy spirit of God coming down upon me.
Spirit of God, what name can I give to Thee?
Joab, I have at times seen a dove hover above its nest,
Hesitating a moment: shall I alight?
Hesitating to alight.
Above my bed the spirit of God was beating its wings,
Coming down nearer and nearer.
Golden dove, I can almost touch and take you with my
     hand.
And I stretched out my arm to the bird;

Then sprang up and pursued it from hall to hall,
To the steep stair that mounts to the palace gardens.
It was growing larger, flashing like a thunderbolt;
At times alighting—
But then suddenly my knees would weaken,
And when I was about to catch him, my whole soul
    would take fright,
And he was gone again, hopping from step to step;
I wanted to take him and dared not. . . .
To whatever place you mount, O dove,
There I shall wait. . . .

There was a little terrace,
A secret one that I believe I did not know before.
The bird of God was suddenly in the open air;
And it seemed suddenly that with it went all my desire.
It would soon be the hour when the sky awakes,
And the wall turns blue;
The gardens below me were deep basins of shadow
Wherein my lucid glance plunged through the mist.
Whose gardens are these, Joab? I do not know;
But I know that here my palace ends.
I leaned out, for I could yet hardly distinguish
What white thing I saw fluttering deep in one garden.
Where the mist was thickest, I felt there was a foun-
    tain;
And beside the fountain, a form leaning.
Was it a woman, veiled?
Or a white wing by the water? . . .

Yes, it fluttered, it palpitated like a wing;
For a moment I thought I had found my bird again.
The sun rising forced me to close my eyes;
When I opened them again, I was dazzled with light,
But only a woman was there.
She had laid aside her veils;
Her bare feet were already in the water.
She went in among the reeds
To the very heart of the fountain.
She went deeper still into my heart.
As she stood there leaning down,
I could not see her face at all,
And her hair covered her shoulders with darkness;
But among the reeds I saw her belly throbbing;
A flower seemed to open between
Her knees when she disjoined them. . . .
My heart within me mounted to my throat,
About to burst in a cry. . . .

[*Re-enter the* SERVANT *who had carried the message to the Hittite.*]

SERVANT: Master, Uriah sends word to the King, his
           master—

DAVID: He isn't coming? . . .

SERVANT: He says: 'Shall I then go into the King's pal-
           ace,
     And Rabbah is not yet taken—'

DAVID: Good. If he does not wish to come, I shall go to
           him.

Go, Joab. Tell him to prepare a very simple meal
And this evening I shall be his guest.
[*Exit* Joab.]

SCENE II

─────────────

David *is seated, anxious;* Joab *standing, listening to him.*
David:　He lives in a little garden. . . .
The meal awaited me under the trellis; the table was
　　white.
"See my vines," he said to me, "what shade they make."
And the shade on the table was charming.
"The bit of wine I own comes from them;
Have some, King David; it is mild, taste it"—
And his wife, just coming in
(Her name is Bathsheba),
Leaned down and filled my cup.
I did not recognize her.
At first I did not even recognize the garden.
Dressed as she was, she seemed much more beautiful.
The dark wave of her hair
Seemed to palpitate about her.
Her face I had never seen was smiling. . . .
But the garden, Joab! What should I say of the garden?
It was no longer like the one that morning
Filled with mist:
It was a quiet spot. . . . I drank the cup of wine.

117

I have drunk many wines, Joab, but that wine,
I believe I had been thirsting for it long before;
It went through me like a deep happiness;
It filled my heart like the fulfillment of prayer.
I felt the strength of my loins renewed.
Bathsheba was smiling; the garden was filled with
     light.
Everything was radiant with love and Uriah's happi-
     ness.

"This is all my happiness, King David," he said; "it is
     simple.
It is held in the hollow of a garden;
It is held in the hollow of the outer walls
Of your palace.
Against the cold and wind your palace protects me
And is not even aware. . . .
I am but one of the least of your men;
Great King David, what am I before you?"

"But your strength protects me against the Philistines,"
I said to him; "what am I before God, Hittite?
I do know you; you are one of the most valiant of my
     men,
And from high in the palace I singled out your garden;
It was pale and blue with the mists of morning;
The sun was hardly risen. . . .
I had not been able to sleep, that night,
And I had prayed so long that I was drunk;

I stumbled at every step mounting the stair;
As if, still asleep, I was pursuing a dream
And dreaming of a marvelous bird, that flew
From hall to hall, and I was tired from following it;
But no doubt, by that dream, God led me
To that terrace,
See! the one you can see yonder.
From there I saw my bird in your garden, Uriah,
When the sun had cleared away the mist;
Yes, the bird I was pursuing— Why do you smile?
It was over there—come, show me, near a spring;
It had parted the reeds,
And there, quietly,
Sheltered from all eyes, so it thought,
It was bathing
In the trembling water. . . .
You were away at the siege of Rabbah, dear Uriah,
You could not have seen it;
But perhaps Bathsheba—?"

Bathsheba was silent, blushing;
And leaning toward the water
To hide her shame, or laughter, she let fall
Over her face her hair.
The day was dying now, the whole garden was bathed
    in shadow. . . .
"Uriah," I said, "why did you not come to the palace?
Was it because Nathan—" "I have not seen Nathan,
    Sire;

119

Not since my return from the siege of Rabbah.

King David, King David! Proud Rabbah is not yet
    taken!

Should I repose in the King's palace

And your people live in expectation!

No! So long as your warriors, O King,

Languish on the wrong side of the walls,

My place is in the camp, among them.

I shall go back this evening."

"Stay with us yet awhile, Uriah;

How long does it take to reach Rabbah? Only a few
    hours—"

Night was already coming on; and now we sat in si-
    lence;

The sky was so clear you could hear the fountain mur-
    muring,

And the darkness, about Uriah, seemed a quiet deep-
    ening of his happiness. . . .

But desire, Joab, desire enters the soul

Like a hungry stranger.

JOAB: Well, King David, who would restrain you? Take
    this woman.

DAVID: Yes. That is just what I did, Joab, at once.

All he possesses is a little garden.

The least of my terraces is larger!

My hands are already so filled with goods

And happiness they cannot hold another grain,

Yet for that bit of happiness

120

I would let all the rest fall to the earth. . . .
It is made of so little!
It seemed that I had only to lift my hand,
Only to want it, to have it;
Only to lay my hand upon it, to take it. . . .

JOAB: You mean Bathsheba, my lord?

DAVID: Yes, Bathsheba. Well, I thought she was more
      beautiful.
She looked better in her garden
When she was bathing naked in the spring.
Bathsheba! Bathsheba. . . . Are you woman? Or
      spring?
O vague object of my desire.
When at last, Joab, I held her in my arms,
Would you believe it, I almost doubted whether it were
      she I desired,
Or whether it was not perhaps the garden. . . .
Or the wine! The wine that I drank,
The wine from his little vineyard!
Did I drink all he had? I fear that I did.
That wine is what I thirsted for, I tell you;
It seemed to touch, and moisten drop by drop
An arid corner of my heart.
You remember: the water of Bethlehem
That Uriah fetched for me one day to stop my fe-
      ver;
That water alone could slake my thirst; no other:
Now I am thirsting for a happiness like Uriah's,
It must be made of little. . . .

Come, Joab, enough! You see it is impossible.
How could I ever possess little enough?
Take this woman away now,
Back to the Hittite's little garden.
All would be well if I desired nothing but her;
But— And besides, I remember, tonight he is coming
    home.
He will find all his happiness tranquil
As he left it; at least he will think so;
For the trace of a ship on the water,
Or of man on the deep body of woman,
God Himself would not recognize it, Joab.
But, Joab, take care that Nathan the prophet know it
    not.
[*Exit* JOAB.]

SCENE III

———————

Same hall in the palace. KING DAVID *is alone, in darkness.*
DAVID: Is it you, Joab! . . . No. It's nothing again.
So must I stay alone until dawn?
Will this night, this night never end!
I prayed, and hoped to fall asleep afterwards;
Will there ever again be any sleep for David?
I tried to pray, but instead fell into thought. . . .
An act in the light of the sun, to the eyes of the flesh,
    may seem beautiful,

122

But woe to him who in darkness looks back with the
    eyes of the spirit!
Woe to him who may not sleep at the top of an action
    done . . .
But in darkness endlessly calls it to mind,
As a blind man caresses with his hands to recognize
The face of a dead friend whom he loved.
Shall I find rest anywhere? Joab! God save us
From nights occupied with neither sleep nor love.

All was ready to let me sleep; all was quiet
And already all was asleep, at heart,
On earth and in heaven
And I was going to sleep. . . . Then the Hittite came.
He came out of the night, suddenly; I hardly recog-
    nized him;
Only the lamp that wakes beside my bed shone on him.
How did he come in? The palace doors are locked.
He stood before me in silence, without removing his
    cloak.
"Uriah," I said, "is it you? Answer me! Why have you
    come? What have you come for?
Has my army triumphed at Rabbah? Surely not.
I should know it already. . . . Take off your cloak.
    I cannot see your eyes. Speak to me.
Speak, I say! Why are you standing motionless?
Who let you come in? What do you want?
Your Bathsheba is waiting for you. Your place is in her
    bed, beside her,

123

In your own garden. Go away, go back to her. I want
    to sleep."

Why did he stand and say nothing?
What did he want of me? Not gifts. He has always re-
    fused them. . . .
He would not even drink
The cup of sweet wine I offered, seeing him stay.
And his presence in the night was prolonged;
Sometimes it seemed to me the lamp beside my bed
    was going out,
Or that the Hittite was withdrawing in the
    shadow. . . .

I do not know whether he had gone when the prophet
    Nathan appeared. . . . Ah! I shall not sleep this
    night. . . .
I had told you Nathan was to be feared! . . .
But now I ask God, Joab, what can man do
If behind every one of his desires God is hidden?

As if he tore each of his words out of myself,
In the night Nathan began to speak.
Oh, what he said! I wish I could blot out his words
    within me. . . .
He told of a poor man who had nothing save one ewe.
"One ewe, I tell you, which he had bought and nour-
    ished,
And watched it grow. He loved it, and it lay in his
    bosom."

124

"No more, Nathan! I know; her name is Bathsheba.
Say no more." But, as if he had not heard me, he con-
tinued:

"Near the poor man lived a very rich man,
Who possessed goods in such great number
And such cattle as could not be counted.
A traveler came to the rich man—"

"No more, Nathan! No more! In him I see my own desire. . . ."

"He was hungry."

"I did not know how to feed my desire."

"But the rich man, who possessed goods in such great
number—"

"Nothing that I had any longer satisfied it."

"Seemed to close his eyes to his own goods,
And took the goods of the poor man."

"But that was what the traveler demanded;
Nothing else, I tell you, could have satisfied him."

It would have been vain to try to silence him;
He spoke out as loud as a king in the house:
"He took the poor man's ewe that was all he had."

"No more, Nathan! No more! . . . The rich man shall
  surely die!"

"He took the poor man's ewe that was all he had—"

"Even that is not what my wayward desire wanted. . . .
See! I gave him back his Bathsheba.
I desired her only in the shade of her garden.
What I desired was Uriah's peace
Among those simple things he left behind
To serve me. . . .
I am willing to repent, but what have I done?
In the time of my desire, Bathsheba
Whirled before my eyes and was all I could see,
But now—" Is that you, Joab?
[*Enter* JOAB; *he stands erect in the darkness, before the
door, without speaking.*]

                              Yes, it is you
At last! I was as impatient for you as for the dawn.
Have you come from Rabbah? Did the Hittite come
  with you?
Is the city taken? No. Otherwise you would have told
  me already.
What happened there? Did you carry out all my or-
  ders?
Didn't I tell you—Uriah was among the brave;
Since he was the most courageous, he should be in the
  front rank. . . .
Why are you silent? . . . Did you urge him forward
  close to the walls?

Too close . . . then, the rest of you retreating, leave
    him there. . . .

Silence, Joab! God Himself must not hear that,

And I must not know it, for fear I may never forget it
    again. . . .

No! No! Tell me he is sleeping in his garden, among
    his vines!

[*Dawn is beginning to make its way into the palace, shining dimly on* JOAB; *behind him, vaguely seen, is a veiled woman.*]

What is this you are trailing after you, in the dark,
    all in mourning?

                 Bathsheba! . . .

Go away! Take her away! I told you, I wish to see her
    no more. . . .

             I hate her!

      END

Philoctetes

OR

The Treatise on Three Ethics

1898

TO MARCEL DROUIN

CHARACTERS

NEOPTOLEMUS

ULYSSES

PHILOCTETES

ACT I

A level waste of snow and ice; a low gray sky.

SCENE I

[Ulysses and Neoptolemus]

NEOPTOLEMUS: Everything is ready, Ulysses. The boat
is moored. I left it in deep water, sheltered on the north,
for fear the wind might freeze the sea around it. This
island is so cold it seems to be inhabited by nothing but
birds along the sea cliffs; but I took the precaution to
tie up the boat in a spot where no one passing along
the coast could see it.

My mind too is made up; it is ready for sacrifice.
Speak now, Ulysses, and tell me; all is ready. For four-
teen days, you have been leaning on the oars or the
tiller, perfectly silent except for the sharp words of
command needed to steer us out of danger of waves.
Faced with your obstinate silence, I soon ceased to
ask questions; I understood that a great sadness was
oppressing your dear spirit, because you were taking

131

me toward death. And I fell silent too, feeling that all
our words were too quickly swept away by the wind
over the immensity of the sea. I waited. I saw the beautiful shore of Skyros falling way behind us, beyond the
horizon of the sea; then the islands of golden sand or
stone, which I loved because I thought they were like
Pylos; thirteen times I saw the sun go down in the sea;
and each morning it rose from paler waves, mounted
less high, more slowly, until at last, on the fourteenth
morning, we waited for it in vain; and ever since then
we have been living, as it were, beyond night and day.
We have seen ice floating on the sea, and were unable
to sleep because of the constant pale glimmer; the only
words I heard from you then were those that signaled
icebergs to be avoided by the stroke of an oar. But
speak now, Ulysses! My spirit is prepared, not like the
goats of Bacchus led to the sacrifice covered with festal
ornaments, but like Iphigenia advancing to the altar,
simple, decent, and unadorned. To be sure, since, like
her, I wish to die for my country without complaint, I
should have preferred to die among the Greeks, in a
land bright with sunshine, and to show, by accepting
death, all my respect for the gods and all the beauty of
my spirit; it is valiant and has not fought. It is hard to
die without glory. Yet, O gods! I hold no bitterness;
though reluctantly, I have left everything, men, sun-
warmed shores . . . and now, coming to this inhospi-
table island, with no trees, no sunlight, where every

green thing is covered with snow, where everything is frozen, and the sky so blank, so gray, it is like another plain of snow stretched above us, far away from everything . . . this seems like death already, here; every hour my mind has been growing so much colder, and purer, all passion gone, that now nothing is left but for the body to die.

Ulysses, at least tell me that Zeus, mysterious Zeus, will be appeased by my faithful death and will give victory to the Greeks; at least you will tell them, won't you, Ulysses! tell them that is why I died without fear . . . you will tell them . . .

ULYSSES: Child, you are not here to die. Don't smile. Now I can tell you. Listen to me and don't interrupt. Would that the gods might be satisfied simply by the sacrifice of one of us! What we have come here to do, Neoptolemus, is not so easy as dying. . . .

This island that looks deserted to you is not so at all. It is inhabited by a Greek; his name is Philoctetes, and your father loved him. Long ago he set sail with us in the fleet that left Greece for Asia, full of hope and pride; he was the friend of Hercules, and one of the noblemen among us; if you had lived in camp before now, you would already know his story. In those days everyone admired his courage; later on they all called it rashness. It was what moved him once when we rested our oars at an unknown island. The shore had a strange aspect; bad omens had undermined our courage. The gods had ordered us to make sacrifice on this island, so Calchas told us, but each one of us was waiting for some other to make the first move; then Philoctetes volunteered, with a smile. On the shore of the island a treacherous snake bit him. Philoctetes was still smiling when he came back on board and first showed us his little wound, just above his foot. It grew worse. Philoctetes soon stopped smiling; his face turned pale, then his troubled eyes filled with an astonished anguish. After a few days his swollen foot stiffened; and he, who had never complained, began to groan pitifully. At first everyone gathered around, eager to console and amuse him; nothing could do so, except to cure him; and, when it was proved that the art of Machaon had no power over his wound, since his cries were likely to weaken our courage, and since the ship was approaching another island, this one, we left him here, alone with his bow and arrows, which are our business today.

NEOPTOLEMUS: What, Ulysses! You left him? Alone?

ULYSSES: Of course, if he had been going to die, I think we might have kept him a little while longer. But no: his wound is not mortal.

NEOPTOLEMUS: But even so?

ULYSSES: Well, do you think the courage of a whole army should have been subjected to the suffering and wailing of a single man? It is easy to see that you never heard him!

NEOPTOLEMUS: Were his cries frightful?

ULYSSES: No, not frightful: plaintive, dampening our souls with pity.

NEOPTOLEMUS: Couldn't someone at least stay and take care of him? What can he do, sick and alone here?

ULYSSES: He has his bow.

NEOPTOLEMUS: His bow?

ULYSSES: Yes: the bow of Hercules. And then I must tell you, child: his rotting foot filled the whole ship with the most unbearable stench.

NEOPTOLEMUS: Ah?

ULYSSES: Yes. And he was obsessed with his illness, incapable ever again of any devotion to Greece. . . .

NEOPTOLEMUS: Too bad. And now we have come, Ulysses. . . .

ULYSSES: Listen again, Neoptolemus: you know Troy has long been condemned; you know how much blood has been spilled, how much virtue, patience, and courage spent there, far from home and our dear land. . . . Well, none of all that has sufficed. Through the priest Calchas the gods have finally declared that the bow and arrows of Hercules alone, in one final test of virtue, could give the victory to Greece. That is why we two have come; blessed be the fate that chose us! And now it seems that on this distant island, all passion put behind us, our great destinies at last are to be resolved, and our hearts, here, more completely dedicated, are at last to achieve the most perfect virtue.

135

NEOPTOLEMUS: Is that all, Ulysses? And now, after such a fine speech, what do you plan to do? My mind still refuses to understand your words completely. . . . Tell me: why have we come here?

ULYSSES: To take the bow of Hercules; now do you understand?

NEOPTOLEMUS: Is that your idea, Ulysses?

ULYSSES: Not mine; it is one the gods put into me.

NEOPTOLEMUS: Philoctetes will not want to let us have it.

ULYSSES: Therefore we shall take it by trickery.

NEOPTOLEMUS: Ulysses, you are detestable. My father taught me never to use trickery.

ULYSSES: It is stronger than force; force doesn't know how to wait. Your father is dead, Neoptolemus; I am alive.

NEOPTOLEMUS: Weren't you saying that it is better to die?

ULYSSES: Not better; it is easier to die. Nothing is worse for Greece.

NEOPTOLEMUS: Ulysses! Why did you choose me? Why did you need me for this act? My whole soul disapproves it.

ULYSSES: Because I cannot do it myself; Philoctetes knows me too well. If he sees me alone, he will suspect some trick. Your innocence will protect us. You must be the one to do this act.

NEOPTOLEMUS: No, Ulysses; by Zeus, I will not do it.

ULYSSES: Child, do not speak of Zeus. You don't understand me. Listen. Do you think I am less sad than you
because my tormented soul is masked, and accepts?
You do not know Philoctetes; he is my friend. It is
harder for me than for you to betray him. The gods'
commands are cruel; they are the gods. I did not talk
to you in the boat because my great saddened heart
no longer even dreamed of words. . . . But you flare
up as your father used to and no longer listen to reason.

NEOPTOLEMUS: My father is dead, Ulysses; do not speak
of him; he died for Greece. Ah, to struggle, suffer, die
for her! Ask whatever you will of me, but not to betray my father's friend!

ULYSSES: Child, listen and answer me: are you not the
friend of all the Greeks rather than the friend of a
single one? Or, rather, isn't our country greater than
one man? And could you bear to save one man if, to
save him, Greece must be lost?

NEOPTOLEMUS: It is true, Ulysses, I could not bear it.

ULYSSES: And you agree that, though friendship is a very
precious thing, our land is still more precious? . . .
Tell me, Neoptolemus, what is virtue?

NEOPTOLEMUS: Teach me, wise son of Laertes.

ULYSSES: Calm your passion; put duty above everything. . . .

NEOPTOLEMUS: But what is duty, Ulysses?

ULYSSES: The voice of the gods, the order of the city,
giving ourselves to Greece; just as we see lovers looking

about them for the most precious flowers as gifts for
their mistresses, and wanting to die for them, as if the
unhappy things had nothing better to give than themselves, what is there too dear for you to give to your
country if it is dear to you? And didn't you agree awhile
ago that friendship came next after your country? What
did Agamemnon have dearer than his daughter, except
his country? You must sacrifice, as on an altar . . .
but now, in the same way, what does Philoctetes have,
living all alone on this island, what does he have more
precious than this bow to give to his country?

NEOPTOLEMUS: Well, in that case, Ulysses, ask him.

ULYSSES: He might refuse. I do not know what mood he
is in, but I do know that his abandonment angered him
against the leaders of the army. It may be he has
angered the gods with his thoughts and, shockingly,
no longer wishes us victory. And maybe the offended
gods have decided to punish him again, through us.
If we force virtue upon him by obliging him to give
up his weapons, the gods will be less severe with
him.

NEOPTOLEMUS: But, Ulysses, can deeds we do against
our will be praiseworthy?

ULYSSES: Don't you think, Neoptolemus, that what is
most important of all is that the gods' orders be carried
out? Even if it must be done without everybody's
consent?

NEOPTOLEMUS: All you said before, I approve; but now

I no longer know what to say, and it even seems to me—

ULYSSES: Shsh! Listen. . . . Don't you hear something?

NEOPTOLEMUS: Yes: the sound of the sea.

ULYSSES: No. It's he! His frightful cries are just beginning to reach us.

NEOPTOLEMUS: Frightful? On the contrary, Ulysses, I hear singing.

ULYSSES [*listening closely*]: It's true, he is singing. He's a good one! Now that he's alone, he sings! When he was with us, he screamed.

NEOPTOLEMUS: What is he singing?

ULYSSES: I can't yet make out the words. Listen: he's coming nearer.

NEOPTOLEMUS: He has stopped singing. He is standing still. He has seen our tracks in the snow.

ULYSSES [*laughing*]: And now he is beginning to scream again. Ah, Philoctetes!

NEOPTOLEMUS: It's true, his cries are horrible.

ULYSSES: Look, run put my sword on that rock, so he will recognize a Greek weapon and know the tracks he has seen are those of a man from his own country. —Hurry, he is getting near.—Good.—Now come; let's post ourselves behind this mound of snow, so we can see him without being seen. How he will curse us! "Beggars," he will say, "perish the Greeks who abandoned me here! Commanders of the army! You liar, Ulysses! You, Agamemnon, Menelaus! May they all

139

be devoured by my disease! Oh, death! Death, I call
on you every day, will you not hear my complaint?
Will you never come? O caves! Rocks! Promontories!
Mute witnesses of my suffering, will you never—"
[*Enter* PHILOCTETES; *he sees the helmet and weapons
placed in the center of the stage.*]

SCENE II

[PHILOCTETES, ULYSSES, NEOPTOLEMUS]

PHILOCTETES: [*He is silent.*]

ACT II

SCENE I

[ULYSSES, PHILOCTETES, NEOPTOLEMUS]

[*All three are sitting.*]

PHILOCTETES: I tell you, Ulysses, only since I have lived apart from men do I understand what is called virtue. The man who lives among others is incapable, believe me, incapable of a pure and really disinterested action. You, for instance—came here—for what?

ULYSSES: Why to see you, my dear Philoctetes.

PHILOCTETES: I don't believe a word of it, but no matter; it is a great pleasure to see you again, and that is enough. I have lost the talent for seeking the motives of what people do, since my own are no longer secret. To whom would I need to appear what I am? My only care is to be. I have stopped groaning, because I knew there was no ear to hear me; I have stopped wishing, because I knew that I could get nothing by it.

ULYSSES: Why didn't you stop groaning sooner, Philoctetes? We might have kept you with us.

PHILOCTETES: That is just what should not have hap-

141

pened, Ulysses. In the presence of others my silence
would have been a lie.

ULYSSES: Whereas here?

PHILOCTETES: My suffering no longer needs words to
make itself known, being known only to me.

ULYSSES: So, you have been silent ever since we left,
Philoctetes?

PHILOCTETES: Not at all. But since I no longer use my
complaint to manifest my suffering, it has become
beautiful, so beautiful that it consoles me.

ULYSSES: Good, my poor Philoctetes.

PHILOCTETES: Above all, don't pity me! I stopped wishing, as I was telling you, because I knew that I could
get nothing by it. . . . I could get nothing from others,
it is true, but a great deal from myself; it was then that
I began to desire virtue; my spirit is now wholly occupied with that, and I am at peace, despite my pain.
At least I was at peace when you came. . . . Why do
you smile?

ULYSSES: I see that you have been busy.

PHILOCTETES: You listen but do not understand me.
Don't you love virtue?

ULYSSES: Yes: my own.

PHILOCTETES: What is it?

ULYSSES: You would listen but would not understand
me. . . . Let's talk about the Greeks instead. Has your
solitary virtue made you forget them?

PHILOCTETES: So as not to be angry with them, yes indeed.

ULYSSES: You hear, Neoptolemus! So our success in the battle which—

PHILOCTETES: —made you leave me here—what do you expect me to think of it, Ulysses? You left me here so as to conquer, didn't you? Then I hope for your sake that you are conquerors. . . .

ULYSSES: And if not?

PHILOCTETES: If not, then we have believed Hellas greater than she was. On this island, you know, I have become every day less Greek, every day more a man. . . . Yet when I see you, I feel— Is Achilles dead, Ulysses?

ULYSSES: Achilles is dead; my companion here is his son. Why, you are sobbing, Philoctetes? . . . Where is the calm you have been seeking? . . .

PHILOCTETES: Achilles! . . . Child, let me stroke your fine forehead. . . . It has been a long time, a long time since my hand touched a warm body; even the birds I kill fall in the water or the snow, and when my hands reach them, their bodies are as cold as those upper regions of the atmosphere where they fly. . . .

ULYSSES: You express yourself well for one who is in pain.

PHILOCTETES: Wherever I go, always, I am a son of Greece.

ULYSSES: But you have no one to talk to here.

PHILOCTETES: Didn't you understand me? I told you that I express myself better now that I no longer talk with men. Except for hunting and sleeping, my whole occupation is thinking. In this solitude nothing, not even pain, interferes with my ideas; and they have taken a course so subtle that I follow them sometimes myself only with difficulty. I have come to understand more of the secrets of life than all my teachers ever revealed to me. I tried telling myself of my suffering, and if the sentence were beautiful, I was comforted accordingly; sometimes I even forgot my troubles in telling them. I learned that words are more beautiful when they ask for nothing. With neither ears nor mouths around me, I used only the beauty of my words; I called them out to the whole island, along the beaches; and the island listened and seemed less solitary; nature seemed the image of my distress; it seemed that I was nature's voice and that the mute rocks were waiting for my voice to tell their illnesses; for I learned that everything around me is sick . . . and that this cold is not normal, for I remember Greece. . . . And I gradually got the habit of crying the distress of things, rather than my own; that seemed better, but how can I explain to you? Anyway, their distress and mine were the same and I was comforted. It was in speaking of the sea and the interminable wave that I made my finest phrases. Do you know, Ulysses—O Ulysses!— some were so beautiful that I sobbed with sadness because there was no man to hear them. It seemed to me his soul would have been changed by them. Listen, Ulysses! Listen. No one has heard me yet.

ULYSSES: I see you got the habit of talking without inter-
ruption. Come, recite for us.

PHILOCTETES [*declaiming*]:   The numberless smiling
waves of the sea—

ULYSSES [*laughing*]:   Why, Philoctetes, that's from
Æschylus.

PHILOCTETES: Perhaps. . . . Does that bother you?
[*Continuing*]

Numberless sobbing waves of the sea—
[*Silence.*]

ULYSSES: And then—

PHILOCTETES: I don't know any more. . . . I am mixed
up.

ULYSSES: Too bad! But you can go on another time.

NEOPTOLEMUS: Oh, please go on now, Philoctetes!

ULYSSES: Well! The child was listening to you! . . .

PHILOCTETES: I don't know how to talk, any longer.

ULYSSES [*rising*]:   I will leave you for a moment to collect your thoughts. Good-by, Philoctetes. But tell me:
no captivity is so hard that it doesn't allow some repose, some forgetfulness, some respite, is there?

PHILOCTETES: True, Ulysses; one day I shot a bird and
it fell; my arrow had only wounded it, and I hoped to
revive it. But how could it keep that airy emotion that
made it fly, down here on this hardened earth where
the cold fixes even upon water, when it freezes, the
form of my logical thought. The bird died; I watched
it die in a few hours; to warm it again, I smothered it

with kisses and warm breath. It died of the need to
fly. . . .

It even seems to me, dear Ulysses, that the stream of
poetry, as soon as it leaves my lips, freezes and dies
because it cannot be repeated, propagated, and that
the intimate flame that animates it is steadily shrink-
ing. I shall soon be, though still alive, quite abstract.
Dear Ulysses, the cold is invading me, and I am frightened, for I find beauty in it, even in its rigor.

I walk securely over things, over frozen fluids. I
never dream any more; I only think. I can no longer
taste hope, and for that reason I am never elated. Here,
where everything is hard stone, when I set anything
whatever down—even a seed—I find it again long
afterwards, just as it was; it has never sprouted. Here,
Ulysses, nothing becomes: everything is, everything remains. In short, here one can speculate! I kept the
dead bird; here it is; the freezing air keeps it ever from
rotting. And my acts, Ulysses, and my words, as if they
were frozen in permanence, surround me like rocks
arranged in a circle. And because I find them there
every day, all my passion is quieted, and I feel the
Truth always firmer—and I should wish my actions
likewise always sounder and more beautiful; true,
pure, crystalline, and beautiful; as beautiful, Ulysses,
as those crystals of clear frost through which the sun,
if the sun ever appeared, could be seen whole. I do
not wish to stop a single ray of Zeus; let him transpierce
me, Ulysses, like a prism, and the refracted light make

my acts lovable and beautiful. I should like to achieve the greatest transparency, the clarification of all my opacity; and I should like for you, watching me act, to feel the light yourself. . . .

ULYSSES [*leaving*]: Well, good-by. [*Pointing to Neoptolemus*] Chat with him, he's listening. [*Exit.*]

SCENE II

[PHILOCTETES AND NEOPTOLEMUS]

NEOPTOLEMUS: Philoctetes! Teach me virtue. . . .

ACT III

SCENE I

PHILOCTETES [*entering; overcome with surprise and grief*]: Blind Philoctetes! Recognize your error, weep for your folly! That the sight of Greeks should have stolen your heart. . . . Did I hear rightly? To be sure: Ulysses was sitting there, and near by was Neoptolemus; they didn't know I was there, they didn't even lower their voices; Ulysses was advising Neoptolemus, teaching him to betray me; telling him— You are cursed, Philoctetes! They came only to steal your bow! How they must need it! . . . Precious bow, my only possession, without it— [*Listening intently*] They are coming! Defend yourself, Philoctetes! Your bow is good, your arm is sure. Virtue! Virtue I cherished so much when I was alone! My silent heart had grown calm before they came. Ah, now I know what it's worth, the friendship they offer! Is Greece my country, detestable Ulysses? And you, Neoptolemus. . . . And yet how he listened to me! So gentle! Child—as fair, oh, fairer than your father was fair. . . . How can so pure a forehead conceal such a thought? "Virtue," he said, "Philoctetes, teach me virtue." What did I tell

148

him? I don't remember anything but him. . . . But
what does it matter now, whatever I told him! . . .
[*Listening*] Footsteps! . . . Who is it coming? Ulysses!
[*Seizing his bow*] No, it's—Neoptolemus.
[*Enter* NEOPTOLEMUS.]

SCENE II

[PHILOCTETES AND NEOPTOLEMUS]

NEOPTOLEMUS [*calling*]: . . . Philoctetes! [*Coming,
nearly fainting*] Ah! I'm sick.
PHILOCTETES: Sick?
NEOPTOLEMUS: You are the cause of my trouble. Make
me calm again, Philoctetes. All you told me has taken
root in my heart. While you were talking, I did not
know what to answer. I listened, and my heart opened
naïvely to your words. Ever since you stopped, I have
kept on listening. But now I am troubled, and waiting.
Speak! I have not heard enough. . . . What were you
saying? A man must devote himself—
PHILOCTETES [*unresponsive*]: —devote himself.
NEOPTOLEMUS: But that is what Ulysses teaches me too.
Devote himself to what, Philoctetes? He says, to one's
country—
PHILOCTETES: —to one's country.
NEOPTOLEMUS: Ah, tell me, Philoctetes; you must go on
now.

PHILOCTETES [*evasive*]: Child—do you know how to draw the bow?

NEOPTOLEMUS: Yes. Why?

PHILOCTETES: Could you string this one?

NEOPTOLEMUS [*disconcerted*]: You mean— I don't know. [*Trying it*] Yes, perhaps.—You see!

PHILOCTETES [*aside*]:   What ease! He is like—

NEOPTOLEMUS [*uncertain*]:   And now—

PHILOCTETES: I have seen all I wanted to see. [*He takes the bow.*]

NEOPTOLEMUS: I don't understand you.

PHILOCTETES: No   matter,   alas! . . . [*Changing his mind*] Listen, child. Don't you believe the gods are above Greece, more important than Greece?

NEOPTOLEMUS: No, by Zeus, I don't believe it.

PHILOCTETES: But why not, Neoptolemus?

NEOPTOLEMUS: Because the gods I serve serve Greece.

PHILOCTETES: So! You mean they are subject?

NEOPTOLEMUS: Not subject—I don't know how to say it. . . . But look! You know they are unknown outside Greece; Greece is their country as well as ours; by serving her, I serve them; they are no different from my country.

PHILOCTETES: Yet, look, I have something to say, there; I no longer belong to Greece, yet—I serve them.

NEOPTOLEMUS: You think so? Ah, poor Philoctetes! Greece is not so easily shaken off . . . and even—

PHILOCTETES [*attentive*]:   And even—?

NEOPTOLEMUS: Ah, if you knew. . . . Philoctetes—

150

PHILOCTETES:　If I knew—what?

NEOPTOLEMUS [*recovering*]:　No, you, you must talk; I came to listen, and now you question me. . . . I see plainly that Ulysses' virtue and yours are not the same. . . . You used to speak so well, but now when you have to speak, you hesitate. . . . Devote oneself to what, Philoctetes?

PHILOCTETES:　I was going to say: to the gods. . . . But the truth is, Neoptolemus, there is something above the gods.

NEOPTOLEMUS:　Above the gods!

PHILOCTETES:　Yes. I will not act like Ulysses.

NEOPTOLEMUS:　Devote oneself to what, Philoctetes? What is there, above the gods?

PHILOCTETES:　There is— [*Taking his head in his hands, overcome*] I don't know any longer. I don't know. . . . Ah! Ah, oneself! . . . I don't know how to say it any longer, Neoptolemus. . . .

NEOPTOLEMUS:　Devote oneself to what? Tell me, Philoctetes.

PHILOCTETES:　Devote oneself—devote—

NEOPTOLEMUS:　You are weeping!

PHILOCTETES:　Child! Ah, if I could only *show* you virtue. . . . [*Standing up suddenly*] I hear Ulysses! Good-by. . . . [*Going*] Shall I ever see you again? [*Exit.*]

NEOPTOLEMUS:　Farewell, Philoctetes.

[*Enter* ULYSSES.]

SCENE III

———————————————

[ULYSSES AND NEOPTOLEMUS]

ULYSSES: Did I come in time? What did he say? Did you talk well, my scholar?

NEOPTOLEMUS: Thanks to you, better than he. But what does it matter? Ulysses—he gave me his bow to string!

ULYSSES: His bow! What irony! Well, why didn't you keep it, son of Achilles?

NEOPTOLEMUS: What good is a bow without arrows? While I had the bow, he wisely kept the arrows.

ULYSSES: Our friend is clever! . . . Does he suspect, do you think? What did he say?

NEOPTOLEMUS: Oh, nothing, or almost.

ULYSSES: And did he recite his virtue to you again?

NEOPTOLEMUS: He talked so well awhile ago; but when I questioned him, he shut up.

ULYSSES: You see! . . .

NEOPTOLEMUS: And when I asked him what else there is to devote oneself to except Greece, he said—

ULYSSES: What?

NEOPTOLEMUS: He didn't know. And when I said that even the gods, as you taught me, are subject to Greece, he answered: then, above the gods, there is—

ULYSSES: What?

NEOPTOLEMUS: He said he didn't know.

152

ULYSSES: Well! Now you see, Neoptolemus! . . .

NEOPTOLEMUS: No, Ulysses, it seems to me now that I understand it.

ULYSSES: You understand what?

NEOPTOLEMUS: Something. Because, after all, on this solitary island, when we were not here, what was Philoctetes devoted to?

ULYSSES: Why, you have already said it: to nothing. What good is solitary virtue? Despite what he believes, it was dissipated, to no use. What good are all his phrases, however fine? . . . Did they convince you? Nor me either.

The reason he was left here, alone on this island, as I have already proved to you, was to rid the army of his groaning and his stench; that is his first devotion; that is his virtue, whatever he may say. His second virtue will be, if he is so virtuous, to be consoled when he loses his bow, by remembering that it was done for Greece. What other devotion, if not to one's country, is imaginable? He was waiting, you see, for us to come and give him the chance. . . . But since it is possible he might refuse, we'd better force his virtue, impose the sacrifice on him—and I think the wisest course is to put him to sleep. You see this bottle. . . .

NEOPTOLEMUS: Ah, don't talk so much, Ulysses. Philoctetes was silent.

ULYSSES: That was because he had nothing to say.

NEOPTOLEMUS: And that was why he was weeping?

ULYSSES: He was weeping because he was wrong.

NEOPTOLEMUS: No, he was weeping because of me.

ULYSSES [*smiling*]:   You? . . . What begins as nonsense, we later call virtue, out of pride.

NEOPTOLEMUS [*bursting into sobs*]:   Ulysses! You don't understand Philoctetes. . . .

ACT IV

SCENE I

[PHILOCTETES AND NEOPTOLEMUS]

[PHILOCTETES *is sitting, alone; he seems overcome with grief, or in meditation.*]

NEOPTOLEMUS [*enters, running*]: I must find him in time! . . . Ah, it's you, Philoctetes. Quick, listen to me. What we came here for is shameful; but you must be greater than we are and forgive me. We came—oh, I am ashamed to say it—to steal your bow, Philoctetes!

PHILOCTETES: I knew.

NEOPTOLEMUS: You don't understand me—we came to steal your bow, I tell you. . . . Ah, defend yourself!

PHILOCTETES: Against whom? You, dear Neoptolemus?

NEOPTOLEMUS: Certainly not against me; I love you and am trying to warn you.

PHILOCTETES: And you are betraying Ulysses. . . .

NEOPTOLEMUS: And I am in despair. . . . It's to you I'm devoted. Do you love me? Say, Philoctetes, is that what virtue is?

PHILOCTETES: Child! . . .

NEOPTOLEMUS: Look what I bring you. This phial is

155

meant to put you to sleep. But I give it to you. Here it
is. Is that virtue?—Tell me.

PHILOCTETES: Child! Superior virtue is attained only
step by step; you are trying to make it at a leap.

NEOPTOLEMUS: Then teach me, Philoctetes.

PHILOCTETES: This phial was to put me to sleep, you
say? [*Taking it, looking at it*] Little phial—you, at least,
do not miss your aim! Do you see what I am doing,
Neoptolemus? [*Drinks.*]

NEOPTOLEMUS: What! This is awful, it is—

PHILOCTETES: Go and tell Ulysses. Tell him—he can
come.

[*Exit* NEOPTOLEMUS, *terrified, running, shouting.*]

SCENE II

———————

[PHILOCTETES, THEN ULYSSES AND
NEOPTOLEMUS]

PHILOCTETES [*alone*]:   And you shall admire me, Ulysses;
I want to compel you to admire me. My virtue rises
above yours and you feel yourself diminished. Be
exalted, my virtue! Be content with your own beauty!
Neoptolemus, why did you not take my bow at once?
The more you loved me, the more difficult that was for

you: you were not devoted enough. Take them. . . .
[*Looking about him*] He's gone. . . .

That drink had an awful taste; it turns my stomach
to think of it; I wish it would put me to sleep faster.
. . . Of all devotions the craziest is to be devoted to
others, for then you become their superior. I am devoted, yes, but not to Greece. . . . I regret but one
thing, and that is that my devotion serves Greece. . . .
Yet, no, I don't even regret it. . . . But don't thank
me: I am acting for myself, not for you.—You will
admire me, won't you, Ulysses? Won't you admire me,
Ulysses? Ulysses! Ulysses! Where are you? You must
understand: I am devoted, but not to Greece—to something else, you understand, to something—what? I
don't know. Will you understand? Ulysses! You will
probably think I am devoted to Greece! Ah, this bow
and these arrows will help you to think that! . . .
Where can I throw them? The sea! [*He tries to run,
but falls overcome by the philter.*] I am too weak. Ah,
my head whirls. . . . He is coming. . . .

Virtue! Virtue! Let me find in your bitter name some
exaltation. Could it be I have already drained it all?
My sustaining pride totters and gives way; my life is
leaking out on every side. "Don't leap; don't leap,"
I told him. Whatever we try beyond our strength,
Neoptolemus, that is what we call virtue. Virtue—
I don't believe in it any longer, Neoptolemus. Listen to
me, Neoptolemus! Neoptolemus, there is no virtue.—
Neoptolemus! . . . He can't hear me.

157

[*Overcome, he falls and sleeps. Enter* ULYSSES *and* NE-
OPTOLEMUS.]

ULYSSES [*seeing* PHILOCTETES]:   And now leave me with
him, alone.

[NEOPTOLEMUS *greatly moved, hesitates.*]

Yes! Go, anywhere; run and get the boat ready, if
you wish.

[*Exit* NEOPTOLEMUS. ULYSSES *approaches* PHILOCTETES,
bends down.]

Philoctetes! . . . Can't you hear me, Philoctetes?—
You will never hear me again?—What can I do? I
wanted to tell you—you have convinced me, Philoctetes. I see virtue now; it is so beautiful that in your
presence I no longer dare to act. To me, my duty seems
crueler than yours, because it seems less dignified. Your
bow—I can't, I no longer want to take it: you have
given it.—Neoptolemus is a child: let him obey. Ah,
here he is! [*In a tone of command*] And now, Neoptolemus, take the bow and the arrows and carry them
to the boat.

[NEOPTOLEMUS *approaches* PHILOCTETES *in grief, falls to
his knees, kisses his forehead.*]

I order you to do it. Isn't it enough to have betrayed
me? Do you wish to betray your country as well? Look
how he has devoted himself to his country.

[NEOPTOLEMUS *obediently takes the bow and arrows;
exit.*]

And now farewell, harsh Philoctetes. Did you despise

me very much? Ah, I should like to know. . . . I should like him to know, I think he is admirable—and that—thanks to him, we shall win.

NEOPTOLEMUS [*calling from a distance*]:   Ulysses!

ULYSSES: I'm coming. [*Exit.*]

ACT V

PHILOCTETES *is alone, on a rock. The sun is rising in a perfectly clear sky. Over the sea, in the distance, a boat is moving away.* PHILOCTETES *looks at it, long.*

PHILOCTETES [*murmuring, very calmly*]: They will never come back; they have no more bows to seek. . . . I am happy.

[*His voice has become extraordinarily mild and beautiful; around him flowers are showing through the snow, and birds from heaven come down to feed him.*]

END

King Candaules

A VERSE PLAY IN THREE ACTS

1900

PREFACE TO THE FIRST EDITION

I SHOULD FIRST excuse myself for writing this preface if I were not writing the preface to excuse myself for having written the play. I fully realize that if the play is good, it has no need of a preface to sustain it; and if the play is bad, the greatest mistake, next to having written it, is to try to explain it. Therefore, up to the present, I have denied myself prefaces; and I should certainly continue to do so were it not for the strangeness of this play and the misunderstanding it is liable to bring about.

Not knowing what sort of reception awaits it, I can and indeed must imagine every possibility—must even imagine that it may be applauded. That would be the misunderstanding. For, seeing the noisy success with which the public has greeted the plays of M. Rostand, for instance, I may not pretend for an instant that any applause my play may receive is for its literary merits; rather, if there should be a burst of applause, it will certainly be for that which those who do not applaud will consider scandalous; it will be for that which I should have suppressed in my play, if that had not meant suppressing at the same stroke the whole play, and if I did not believe, as I confess I do, that a dramatic work should offer

163

all sorts of attractions in addition to its deeper meaning, should be a spectacle and a fine spectacle, should not fear to "speak to the senses." But the more this latter aspect of the work, which after all is secondary here, is likely to please the public, the greater is my need to clear myself at once, in order to avoid at least prolonging a misapprehension. But let me explain.

I

I have meant, quite simply, to create a work of art.

But since, today, art no longer exists, and since, anyway, there is no longer anyone who understands it, I am obliged to bring to the fore the part played by ideas, precisely the part that in my eyes is not the most important, the one that must remain, I believe, in the service of beauty, but can only serve beauty if itself is, first of all, perfectly solid and right. Ideas are the skeleton of my drama, but, alas, today it is only of the skeleton that I dare speak.

II

King Candaules was desperately in love with his wife and regarded her as the most beautiful of women. Obsessed by his passion, he was continually boasting of her beauty to Gyges,[1] one of his guards, of whom he was very

[1] Is it really necessary to excuse myself for having strictly followed neither history nor legend? The famous ring of Gyges was not given by Candaules. And it was found, not in a fish, but rather in the cavernous flanks of a great bronze horse, as Plato reports it. Furthermore, Gyges was not a fisherman, but a shepherd. And furthermore, he did not make use of the ring in order to see the Queen. And furthermore, etc., etc.

164

fond and to whom he confided his most important affairs. After a while Candaules (since there was no escaping his misfortune) spoke to Gyges in these terms: "It seems to me that you don't take my word for the beauty of my wife. Speech makes less impression than the sight of things: you must do what you can, then, to see her naked."

"What are you saying, my lord!" cried Gyges. "Have you considered this? Are you ordering a slave to look upon the Queen? Do you forget that a woman puts off her modesty with her dress? The rules of propriety have been known for a long time; they must serve us as a guide. Now, one of the most important of these is: 'Let each look on his own.' I am persuaded that you have the most beautiful of all wives; but I beg you not to require of me so improper a thing."

Thus Gyges refused the King's proposal, fearing its consequences for himself. "Set your mind at rest, Gyges," said Candaules. "Fear neither your King (these words are not a trap to test you) nor the Queen; she will do you no harm. I shall so arrange it that she will not even know that you have seen her. . . ."

There was no way out for Gyges. He or Candaules had to die.

(HERODOTUS: *Clio*, VIII ff.)

III

This play derives, perhaps, simply from a reading of Herodotus; yet somewhat, perhaps, also from the reading of an article in which an author of talent, pleading "for moral freedom," came to the point of blaming the custodians of art, beauty, wealth—in short, the "ruling classes" —for not having the sense to attempt to educate the people by setting up for them exhibitions of certain kinds of beauty. The author did not say—in fact, he was careful not to say—whether the people would have the right to touch it. I imagine, since he is too intelligent not to recognize that there alone the interest of the matter lay, that he had the good sense to prefer to evade the issue, feeling that its consequences were too grave and fearing that he would not be able to demonstrate them. Hence my *Candaules* was born.

And then, before long, this newborn drama grew up and ran away. Other questions arose from the first, as corollaries to it, exactly. If Candaules was too great and too generous,[2] if he forces himself to the extreme in permitting the ignorant Gyges first to see, then to touch and share that which he learns, slowly and all too quickly, to enjoy—then to what point, to what person, can such communism be carried? What will Nyssia think of it? And Candaules himself, afterwards? And Gyges? . . . But here I break off commentary: the play must speak for itself.

Perhaps all we are justified in seeing in this tragic story of Candaules, according to the Greek historian, is the rise of the first of the Mermnades to the throne of

[2] "Generous to the point of vice," wrote Nietzsche; and again: "It is a curious thing to note that excessive generosity does not go without loss of modesty." Modesty is a kind of reserve.

Lydia. And yet perhaps it is not impossible to see in it also the defeat, almost the suicide, of an aristocracy whose too noble qualities first easily undo it and then keep it from defending itself. . . . However that may be, let no one look for "symbols" here, but simply for an occasion to generalize. And may the choice of such a subject, the exceptional character of Candaules, find in the play its explanation and excuse.

IV

In the theater any new character always seems an exceptional character at first. The audience, before it can accept him, must protest. Whatever falls outside the conventions, in the theater, seems false. The theater lives by conventions. We are vexed if anyone frees us from them; or, rather, tries to free us from them. For the audience, there are natural feelings and others that are not. All possible feelings exist in man, but there are certain ones that we exclusively call natural, instead of calling them simply more common. As if the common were more natural than the rare! Lead more natural than gold! Everything Candaules does is natural.

V

Some have reproached me for the coldness, the rapidity, the inelasticity of my play. Some have said that the subject is hinted at rather than treated, or, better, that it is more drawn than painted. That I know, the reproach is just; but at a time when everyone paints, when no one or almost no one any longer draws, I have tried to draw, wishing to leave in the drawing all its probity, its severity, its logic, and to use no technique (which, to my mind, would be too easy) of lyrical overloading and bombast to hide perhaps it faults. If such faults are there, what I wish is that they may be apparent, just as I hope its virtues will also be.

Some have reproached me for using a trick of typography to give the appearance of verse to what is most often only plainly rhythmed prose. I can give no other reason than this: from the moment I conceived the play, it is thus that I wished it to be; and although, afterwards, in order to satisfy a few friends, I put my too free verses end to end and had them copied "as prose," I was never pleased with their new appearance.

CHARACTERS

.

CANDAULES

GYGES

NYSSIA

SEBAS

ARCHELAUS

NICOMEDES

SYPHAX

PHARNACES

PHÆDRUS

SIMMIAS

PHILEBUS

COOK

SERVANTS

ACT I

The scene is one end of a very formal garden set up as a banquet hall. Somewhat to the right, a table covered with all the preparations for a feast.

PROLOGUE

GYGES: Whoever wants to keep his happiness, let him
        hide!
  Or hide his happiness, at least, from others.
  In an hour King Candaules will be here,
  Fattening flatterers at his expense.
  Oh well! I am no good at flattery and fine speech,
  Cleverer with my hands than with my tongue,
  My name is poor man Gyges;
  Only four things in this world are mine to keep:
  My cabin, my fish net, my wife, and my poverty.
  And then a fifth: my strength;
  With that I built my cabin and my pride;
  With that I gathered rushes by the river,
  And covered my house with them;
  When the tide goes out I gather seaweed;
  And when it's dry it makes a sweet-smelling bed;
  Every night, wife and I are tired, and we sleep,

And I am out fishing at dawn,
With my net on one arm and my strength in the other;
Because in the sea, where everything is born,
The fish are fresh and free and belong to no one
Until they are caught.

   I caught this very fish myself.
I caught it, my wife cooked it.
She has worked in the palace kitchens the past **two**
    days.
Open-hearted Candaules, just as if his own happiness
Seemed too much for one man, has called about **him**
The kings and great men of his land;
They have been feasting for the past two days.

   Not long ago, poor man Gyges knew King Candaules.
We are the same age,
And when we both were young,
Little Candaules liked to come down to the seashore,
Where I played; and he played
And wanted me to share in his games.
He had a giving nature.
He no longer remembers, because he is rich,
But in a poor man's life everything stands out.
I have not seen him since that time;
But I love Candaules still, and grieve
To see him surrounded with lords,
All shameful flatterers and fools,
Who profit from his large bounty

And praise him but cannot understand him.
Long live Candaules! All those fine flattering speeches
Are not worth the simple "thank you" they get from
    him.
But what does it matter to Candaules that I love him?
The eyes of the great pass over the small and do not
    see them.
That is why, right now, I am leaving,
Though they did invite me to the kitchens;
But the feast will finish late,
And the drinking later still;
And tomorrow I would miss the tide.

   Come on, proud man Gyges, sober man Gyges,
Go take your wet fish nets from the pantry,
Don't look around too much, just wait at the door
Until your wife has washed the rich men's plates
And joins you to follow you back
To Gyges the fisherman's house. Come, Gyges.
[*Exit* Gyges.]

SCENE I

Enter the cook *and several* servants *laden with platters.*
cook: Put fruit all around . . .

                  Hey, Gyges! Are you leaving?
  No, those salads farther over!

                    Gyges, stay with us!

173

[*Continuing to* GYGES, *who is off stage*]

The King is inviting to the palace all who pass by.

I invite you in the name of the whole kitchen.

The King wants so much wine to be poured tonight

That it will trickle down even to our tables

And the least servant be drunk.

GYGES [*re-enters, carrying his nets*]:   I am not one of the King's servants.

COOK: What does it matter? If his table is too full and overflows, take advantage.

GYGES: I don't like to take advantage of the King.

[*Exit.*]

COOK: What a boor! Fortunately his wife is more amiable.

[*To the servants*] Hurry. Let's hurry.

[*Enter various characters, moving about.*]

SEBAS [*with* ARCHELAUS; *taking a fig and eating it; to the cook*]:   Are we well placed?

[*The cook points to a place.*]

Not too far from the flute girls, remember?

COOK: There won't be any.

SEBAS *and* ARCHELAUS: Oh!

COOK: The Queen doesn't want them.

ARCHELAUS: We shall console ourselves with looking at the Queen.

SEBAS: So she is coming to the banquet?

COOK: This will be the first time she is seen in public.

SEBAS: Why was she hiding? Does she think she is too ugly?

174

ARCHELAUS: No: on the contrary, too beautiful.

SEBAS: What is it? Pride?

ARCHELAUS: No, modesty.

[*Both laugh.*]

SEBAS [*taking more figs, eating, passing some to* ARCHE-
LAUS]:   Wake your appetite!

My dear Archelaus, I am in despair:
She is not staying.

ARCHELAUS: Who?

SEBAS: The kitchen woman.

ARCHELAUS: The wench you had last night?

SEBAS: Her husband is taking her off after supper.

ARCHELAUS: Too bad for you.

SEBAS: Too bad for her, poor thing. . . .
As for the flute girls . . .

[*They move away.*]

ARCHELAUS [*is heard saying*]:   . . . What an ogre!

[NICOMEDES, SYPHAX, *and* PHARNACES]

NICOMEDES: Well, my dear Syphax! This little banquet,
Isn't beginning too badly. What do you think of it?

SYPHAX: I think better of the banquet than of Candaules.

PHARNACES: Yet he is better than the banquet.

NICOMEDES: Do you think so?

PHARNACES: Yes, because the banquet gives us only one
Candaules
Whereas Candaules will give us many banquets.

COOK [*to the serving men*]:   Figs over here.

SYPHAX [*going aside with* NICOMEDES]:   I am beginning
      in fact to fear
   That neither politics nor stupidity
   Makes the King keep us feasting here,
   Loading his kindness on us,
   But rather, as you were telling me,
   A sort of vague generosity.

[NICOMEDES *gestures agreement.*]

COOK: Two cups are missing, there.

SYPHAX [*continuing*]:   And that precisely is what bothers
      me:
   So long as I could have contempt for the King,
   I gladly took his gifts:
   But if he is indeed the man I am beginning to believe,
   I shall now despise myself for taking them.

NICOMEDES: Oh, come now! You take nothing he doesn't
      offer.
   When good things come, from heaven or from men,
   Joyously accept their benefits;
   That is the greatest secret of happiness.

COOK: I think everything is ready.

[*Exit with servants. The nobles move away.*]

      [PHÆDRUS *and* SIMMIAS, *who are friends;
         and* PHILEBUS]

PHÆDRUS: No, believe me, dear Simmias: King Can-
      daules
   Has more wisdom than you grant him,

176

It is great wisdom to consider oneself happy.

SIMMIAS: Is he really happy or does he simply appear
     so?

PHÆDRUS: It takes even more wisdom to appear so.

PHILEBUS: Besides, believing you are happy is better
     than trying to be so.

PHÆDRUS: With all his treasure, he still knows the value
     of friendship;

He knows it is not bought with gold,

And so puts little value upon that

Which flatterers pretend to have for him;

He puts the true price on their words,

And though he may pay for them, he never believes
     them.

More than that, I have never seen him angry

Except with them.

PHILEBUS: If there is anything that hinders his happi-
     ness

It must be this: to know that because of all his wealth

He has about him only courtiers—not one friend.

SIMMIAS: He has his wife.

PHILEBUS: But that is not the same thing.

SIMMIAS: They say he loves her passionately.

PHÆDRUS: And he is not wrong to do so.

SIMMIAS: They say she is extremely beautiful.

PHÆDRUS: But no one has seen her.

SIMMIAS: They say she is to appear at the banquet to-
     night.

PHILEBUS *and* PHÆDRUS: Who said so?

177

[*Meanwhile enter* CANDAULES, *approaching with several of the preceding nobles; he hears the last words.*]

SIMMIAS [*turning toward him*]:   Why, Candaules himself.

SCENE II

KING CANDAULES: Yes, Candaules did say so. Queen
Nyssia
Will adorn the banquet this evening. A splendid eve-
ning—
The beauty of the day has been mounting toward this
hour
Like a hymn of joy rising
Toward some acute vibration
The senses can hardly perceive.
And now all is quiet, the hymn languishes;
But there on the little terrace, not an hour ago,
We were enraptured.
You should have come with us, gentle Philebus;
There the laurels are in flower,
They perfume the darkness. . . .

SYPHAX, NICOMEDES, *and* PHARNACES: . . . Delightful.

KING CANDAULES [*to* PHILEBUS, *who is still with* PHÆDRUS
and SIMMIAS]:   You are intruding on Phædrus
and Simmias.

PHÆDRUS *and* SIMMIAS: Oh, not at all!

178

KING CANDAULES: You see, I do not ask them to follow
  me,

Their friendship looks for solitude, fulfills it.

I envy your friendship, handsome Simmias;

It is more precious than my wealth,

And it is my wish that my wealth protect it.

Sebas, I have had some white figs gathered for you

And brought from far away;

I am glad that your good taste prefers them,

That you find them, as I do, sweeter, more flavorsome.

Pharnaces, your wit is charming;

Tomorrow you will continue that story for me.

The verses you recited me, dear Syphax, are most
  pleasing,

I shall have them set to music. Alas, Archelaus,

Tonight there are no flute girls playing—

The Queen will be here.

If you looked at them as you did yesterday,

Her modesty would take offense.

Gentlemen, I am ashamed to ask this favor of you:

Keep to the strictest decency in your remarks:

The Queen will be here,

In a moment I shall come back with her.

[*Starts away, then turns back.*]

What a splendid evening! . . .

On the terrace, gentle Philebus,

We sipped the sweetest sherbets you can dream
  of. . . .

 Oh the fullness of my happiness!

How could my senses alone ever drain it?
My thanks to you, gentlemen; you will help me use it;
Now, like the juice from grapes, let me squeeze out
All the ecstasy and happiness left in this day's end!
A joy shared with you is doubled.
Tomorrow we shall retell this beautiful day.

[*Exit.*]

SYPHAX: Candaules is marvelous.

ARCHELAUS: He is beautiful.

SEBAS: He is great.

NICOMEDES: The way he receives us is magnificent.

PHARNACES: Yes, truly.

SYPHAX: In a moment we shall drink to Candaules' happiness.

PHARNACES: Syphax, that's dangerous.

SYPHAX: For whom? For me?

PHARNACES: For him.

SYPHAX: Bah! How could misfortune come to him?

NICOMEDES: From his wife, perhaps.

PHÆDRUS: She is the most faithful of wives.

PHILEBUS: Then, from himself.

SIMMIAS: Shsh! Quiet! Here they are.

SCENE III

_____

KING CANDAULES [*to the* QUEEN]:   Remove your veil:
these are all my friends.

THE QUEEN: So many friends, dear lord! I knew you
      were very rich,

  And yet not so much as this.

  Let all be welcome around me

  Since you wish me to be with them at this table.

[*All sit. A certain embarrassment follows on the* QUEEN's
words.]

ARCHELAUS [*to* PHARNACES]:   Say something, come!

PHARNACES [*whispering*]:   I don't know what to say, ex-
      cept that the Queen is very beautiful.

ARCHELAUS [*to* PHILEBUS]:   You, then.

[PHILEBUS *gestures silence.*]

THE QUEEN: What! You are all silent! Is it because of
      me?

  However great my pleasure in gratifying Candaules'
      desire

  That I should sit, as I do now, at this table,

  If I could think

  That the joy of the banquet might be in the least
      hampered,

  I should quit this table on the instant,

  For joy is in its place here

  More than the Queen.

NICOMEDES: I do not dare express to the Queen

  How the extraordinary beauty of her features

  Astonishes us still

  So that our silence is only

  Contemplative admiration.

KING CANDAULES: Quiet, Nicomedes!

That is precisely what the Queen
Feared and would avoid:
To be praised.
Nyssia! Please answer them;
These gentlemen, unless we both take care,
Are likely to give us nothing at this banquet
But a dismal game of well-turned compliments
And remarks with no pluck.
No doubt your unaccustomed presence
Imposes on them some constraint.
I swear that ordinarily they know better how to talk;
I beg you, bring your wit to their aid;
Let it heal the hurt your beauty has done them
And hastily dissipate the boredom beginning to settle
    on them all.

THE QUEEN: If indeed my face is at fault,
   It is easy, my lord, to keep it from doing further dam-
    age.
   Allow me to cover its blushes with a veil,
   Which I shall never lift but by constraint,
   Which should never have been lifted but for you.

KING CANDAULES [*irritated*]:   No, Nyssia, no. . . . A few
    more remarks of this kind
   And all the pleasure of the banquet will be spoiled.
   Take off your veil entirely, Nyssia.
   And let us, gentlemen, in haste,
   Offer our first cup to joy!
   The joy of this feast is still asleep,
   Come! Let the sound of voices wake it up!

[*A stir.*]

Nyssia! You drink too, Nyssia!

SYPHAX: Shall I reply for us all?

VOICES: Yes! Do, Syphax!

KING CANDAULES: First fill your cup.

SYPHAX: For all the friends of Candaules
I offer my cup to the perfect beauty
Of Nyssia, wife of Candaules—

KING CANDAULES: Peace, Syphax!

SYPHAX: And to Candaules too, possessor of so rare a
treasure,
Who does not hide it, nor keep it for himself,
But allows our respectful and charmed eyes to be
dazzled.

SEVERAL VOICES [*raising their cups*]:   Well said! Well
said, Syphax! Long live Candaules!

KING CANDAULES: But no, gentlemen, do not be grateful
to me
For offering at this banquet the beauty of the Queen;
Indeed, to be alone in the enjoyment of her
Has made me suffer much.
The greater my admiration of her,
The more I felt how much I deprived you all.
I seemed a greedy monopolizer
Wrongfully withholding light.

PHARNACES: Wrongfully, Candaules? Is it not right
For every man to dispose of his property as he please?

KING CANDAULES: Perhaps. But I should feel that I was
stealing from you all

Any goods that I alone enjoyed.

SEBAS: One couldn't better express a more admirable
    thought.

THE QUEEN [*to* CANDAULES]:   Fie, my lord! You seem to
    forget

That the property you speak of is myself.

KING CANDAULES: Oh, you mistake my words!

I was no longer thinking of you, Nyssia,

And what I was saying is true

Only in a more general way.

PHILEBUS: But, madam, what do you think of this shar-
    ing?

SIMMIAS: Philebus is certainly bold.

THE QUEEN [*to* PHILEBUS]:   I think there are kinds of
    happiness

One kills in trying to share them.

[*The conversation has gradually become animated, several voices heard at once;* SEBAS, PHÆDRUS, *and the* KING
join in almost simultaneous repartee.]

KING CANDAULES [*annoyed, as if he had heard only the*
    QUEEN's *reply*]:   But that depends on who—

PHÆDRUS [*to* SIMMIAS]:   Did you hear how subtly

The Queen eluded the irony?

SEBAS: One couldn't give a prettier answer

To a more specious question.

KING CANDAULES: Quiet, Sebas! Turn your mind to the
    figs, rather.

[*Throwing him some.*]

Phædrus! You are not drinking! Lift your cup, come!
Gentlemen, I have resolved to test you all.

NICOMEDES: Test us, Candaules? In what way?

KING CANDAULES: With drink.

PHÆDRUS: I am a sorry drinker, drunkenness frightens me.
Do leave me out, Candaules, I beg of you.

KING CANDAULES: Well, Phædrus! what do you fear?
Drunkenness can only manifest
What we have within ourselves.
Why should a man be afraid
Who has but what is noble to be shown?
Drunkenness does not deform, it exaggerates;
Or rather it makes one surrender
What often in excess of modesty he would hide:
You, Phædrus, hide your wisdom; Pharnaces and
    Syphax, their wit;
Archelaus, nothing; Sebas, the figs he is stuffing him-
    self with.

PHÆDRUS: The King is about to talk too much.

KING CANDAULES [*to the servants*]:   Carve this fish.

NICOMEDES: Isn't it golden!

KING CANDAULES: I wager it lived in that part of the sea
Where the summer sun goes down. Just look.

[*The* COOK *shows it.*]

ARCHELAUS: It's superb.

COOK: It's a dolphin.

KING CANDAULES: Let's drink to the luster of this fish,
    gentlemen!

And you Pharnaces, make us some verses on the dolphin—

Come!

PHARNACES: The King no doubt forgets that fish are mute.

SYPHAX: Not all! They say there was one that spoke oracles.

PHARNACES: Then, you may make the verses, Syphax.

SEVERAL VOICES: Verses! Verses!

SYPHAX: Wait—if they are bad, too bad!
    The sun that gilded your fin
    With its sublime rays, dolphin,
    Speaks to him who sees in-
    To your oracles, dolphin!

PHARNACES *and* KING CANDAULES: Bravo, Syphax!

NICOMEDES: Let's hope the fish will be better than the verses.

[*The fish is passed.*]

KING CANDAULES: How is it, Pharnaces, Archelaus?

PHARNACES: Excellent! . . .

ARCHELAUS [*shouting*]:   Hell and the devil! What is this? I almost swallowed a ring.

NICOMEDES [*and others*]:   A ring!

ARCHELAUS: I broke two teeth on it.

SYPHAX [*under his breath*]:   A voracious brute!

ARCHELAUS: It was buried in the flesh of this fish.
    Are you laughing?

SYPHAX [*and others, protesting*]:   Certainly not.

SEBAS: But your bites are too big.

186

ARCHELAUS: I might have been strangled.

SYPHAX: Yes, quite simply.

NICOMEDES: Let's see the ring a moment.

PHILEBUS [*handing it to him*]:   This is quite out of the
  ordinary.

NICOMEDES [*claiming it in his turn*]:   In the fish, you say?

SYPHAX: Strange food.

NICOMEDES: The stone is pretty.

KING CANDAULES: Oh! I see nothing in it but a rather
  ordinary sapphire.

I have several a good deal larger and clearer.

Tomorrow I shall show them to you, Nicomedes.

SYPHAX [*to whom the ring has finally come*]:   And now
  who wants the ring?

ARCHELAUS: The fish gave it to me; I give it to the King.

SYPHAX: Ah, I say! For Archelaus, the remark is well
  turned.

SEVERAL VOICES: To Candaules! Of course. To Candaules!

PHÆDRUS [*taking the ring to pass it back to the* KING]:
  Wait. There is something written here—

NICOMEDES [*leaning over* PHÆDRUS *to look*]:   Syphax was
  right: the dolphin has spoken.

KING CANDAULES *and* NYSSIA: Ah! What does it say?

NICOMEDES: I cannot quite see.

PHÆDRUS: Pharnaces has good eyes.

PHARNACES [*rises and goes to one of the torches, or lamps,
  which servants have meanwhile brought in*]:
  Two words in Greek.

187

KING CANDAULES: Translate for us.

PHARNACES: Εὐτυχίαν κρύπτω.

PHÆDRUS: "I hide happiness."

SEVERAL VOICES: I hide happiness? What happiness? . . .

NICOMEDES: The oracle is not clear.

PHARNACES [*as if seeing something more*]: Wait! Wait. . . .

[*All are in suspense.*]

No. That's all.

King Candaules, I put this mysterious ring on your finger.

KING CANDAULES [*stopping* PHARNACES *with a gesture*]: Cook! Where does this fish come from?

COOK: A man brought it in, awhile ago.

It looked like a fine fish, and I bought it.

KING CANDAULES: Where is the man now?

COOK: He went back home.

KING CANDAULES: Why didn't you keep him in the kitchen this evening for the feast?

COOK: He did not wish to stay.

KING CANDAULES: I don't like to see my offers rejected. . . .

What sort of man was he?

COOK: A poor fisherman, of no account.

KING CANDAULES: And what did you give him for this fish?

COOK: Four pieces of silver.

KING CANDAULES: He deserved gold.

COOK: He's so wretchedly poor that silver was enough.

KING CANDAULES: In the first place, no one is wretchedly
poor in my kingdom—

Or maybe I did not know him.

What is his name?

COOK: His name is Gyges, by your pleasure.

KING CANDAULES: Let him be brought in, I should like
to know him.

I swear, no finger will pass into this ring

Before I have seen this man—

Gyges, you say?

COOK: Yes, Gyges.

KING CANDAULES: —Before I have spoken to Gyges the
fisherman.

Come! Go get him.

COOK [*giving instructions to a man*]:   It will be done at
once.

[*The* KING *is silent, imposing a rather long silence on the
others.*]

SEBAS: It is brighter here than in the hall.

PHILEBUS: This corner of the garden is lovely at night.

NICOMEDES: What a view!

I like this vista stretching to the sea.

There, you see! The delicate crescent of the moon is
rising.

NYSSIA: What is that glimmer of light?

PHILEBUS: Madam, it is the moon.

ARCHELAUS: Oh no! Yonder: just at the edge of the
shore.

PHARNACES: One would think it a cabin burning.

NICOMEDES: Ah! It is beautiful.

SEBAS: These pheasants are exquisite.

ARCHELAUS: I took a quail.

SYPHAX: Candaules says nothing and seems worried.

KING CANDAULES: We can hardly see any longer. Bring
       lights.

[*Torches are brought in.*]

   My cup is empty!

   Yours too, Philebus, Pharnaces! . . . The wine is giv-
       ing out.

[*Wine is offered to* PHILEBUS, *who refuses.*]

   Well! If you will not drink, then talk; I am wor-
       ried.

      Those two words on the ring—what do you think of
          them?

   I cannot take my mind off them.

PHILEBUS: Why, O Candaules?

   These, perhaps, are only words of double meaning,

   Such as the custom is to ascribe to oracles.

   The credence we give them is due solely to their mys-
       tery.

   With great difficulty, in the end we discover

   Under their apparent enigma a plain and well-known
       truth.

PHARNACES: And more often than that, we discover
       nothing at all.

KING CANDAULES: So, according to you, these words
       mean practically nothing?

PHILEBUS: "I hide happiness"? No; nothing.

190

KING CANDAULES: Good! I might have been worried about them.

NICOMEDES: Besides, these words seem to me of a kind
To tax the wits even of a sober man,
And we are none of us, I believe,
In a state to solve enigmas now!

SYPHAX: Well said, Nicomedes!
Let's simply drink to the happiness of Candaules.
He, at least, is not like the ring,
He does not hide his happiness; quite the contrary!

PHARNACES [*rising to toast with the others*]:   To Candaules, the happiest man on earth!

KING CANDAULES [*striking the table violently with his fist*]:   Look here! What do you know of my happiness? Indeed!

PHÆDRUS [*very calm*]:   Nothing, Candaules.

KING CANDAULES [*recovering*]:   Gentlemen, pardon me,
Some strange anxiety
Swept me away. You, Nyssia,
You are silent unless we beg for your words;
Tell me, what do you think of my happiness?

NYSSIA: I think it is like myself, my lord.

KING CANDAULES [*angry again*]:   More enigmas! What do you mean by that?
Come! Speak more clearly.

NYSSIA: I meant to say
That I fear it may fade, from exposure.

KING CANDAULES [*beginning to feel his wine*]:   Then cover yourself!

191

No matter, now that all have seen you.

[NYSSIA *gestures sad astonishment.*]

Oh, Nyssia, pardon me! Ah, what have I said?
Believe me, I had no wish to hurt you. . . .
The truth is, on the contrary, that for me
My happiness seems
To draw its strength, its violence, from others.
It seems to me sometimes that it exists
Only in the knowledge others have of it,
That I truly possess
Only when others know that I possess.
I swear to you, gentlemen, that I should not care
To possess the whole earth
If, to do so, I had to remain alone on earth,
Or likewise if no one knew it.
Gentlemen, please believe me, it is especially
When you partake of my wealth
That I know my wealth.
I am very rich.—No, this wine
Does not make me exaggerate.—
I am very rich.
And I was angry awhile ago
When you drank a toast saying: "Health
To Candaules, the richest man on earth,"
Because, gentlemen,
You still do not know my wealth.

PHÆDRUS: No, it was not to your wealth, Candaules,
No! We drank to your happiness.

192

KING CANDAULES [*rising, excited*]: Well! This is still
    worse!

What do you know of my happiness?

What do I know of it myself?

Is it possible to see one's own happiness?

We see it only in others;

And we feel our own only when we are not looking
    for it.

    The air is lifeless tonight, wearying.

Where is this Gyges? Not here yet?

[KING CANDAULES *rises, leaves his chair, or bench, stag-*
gering, but only slightly.]

Bring me more wine! I want everyone here to be drunk!

We'll get Gyges drunk when he comes.

[*Drink is poured for him; he approaches* PHÆDRUS.]

And you still do not know, Phædrus—a secret—

[*He sits down between* PHÆDRUS *and* SIMMIAS. *The order*
of guests is now somewhat relaxed, as happens, with us,
at coffee after dinner. NICOMEDES *approaches the* QUEEN
and talks with her. KING CANDAULES, *continuing, to* PHÆ-
DRUS]

After all, to me, what does happiness matter?

Only the poor, don't you think,

May rightly be concerned with being happy?

Come, Phædrus, do you understand me,

Does your wisdom endorse

What I can say only to you?

What I mean is that every new gift that comes to us

Brings with it a new desire to test it out—
For me, to possess is to experiment.

[*He taps the table with his empty cup, listening to the sound it makes.*]

Why are you silent, Phædrus? Have you had nothing
    to drink?
Oh, Phædrus, is happiness for you in being calm?
Would you teach us to sleep, not to live?
Am I perhaps wiser than you, O philosopher,
Since I know that wherever happiness abounds,
There life is superabundant.
O Phædrus, when a man is poor
He wears himself out with desire,
Desiring more life, more happiness—
No, not to desire, I say,
No, but to work for what we desire,
And when we possess it—risk it.
Risk it! That is the other form of happiness;
That is the rich man's happiness.
And it is mine.
I am rich, Phædrus! I am alive.

SIMMIAS: If your happiness were in friendship
You would not speak of staking it, Candaules . . .
But friendship is one thing you have never had.

KING CANDAULES: You tell the truth; oh, how many treas-
      ures, good Simmias,
Would I not give for yours?

[*Re-enter the* COOK, *left, bringing* GYGES.]

COOK: King, here is the fisherman.

KING CANDAULES [*seated again on the right-hand side of the table*]:   Ah! Ah! So you are Gyges?

GYGES: Yes, I am Gyges, King Candaules.

KING CANDAULES: Fisherman Gyges?

GYGES: Yes, fisherman Gyges.

KING CANDAULES: Poor man Gyges?

GYGES: Poor man Gyges, King Candaules.

ARCHELAUS: He is scarcely eloquent.

SEBAS: That comes of having to do with fish.

KING CANDAULES: Quiet, Sebas! Come here, Gyges;
Why were you not in the kitchens for the feast?

[GYGES *makes no answer.*]

Someone give him a cup. Do you drink wine, ever?

GYGES: You might say never.

KING CANDAULES: Taste that.

[*Seeing that a servant is about to pour him ordinary wine*]
No! Not that. Pour him the best.

PHARNACES: But this is good, Gyges!

KING CANDAULES: Peace, Pharnaces!
Is it true that you are wretchedly poor, Gyges?

GYGES: No, not wretched—just poor.

KING CANDAULES: Are you very needy?

GYGES: I have what I need.

SYPHAX: He's not too stupid, for a fisherman.

KING CANDAULES: What have you?

GYGES: I had a house;
But my wife came home, King,
A little drunk from your palace,
And tried to stir the fire on our hearth

To heat my evening soup,
And she set fire to some straw.
I don't know how it happened—
The cabin was built of dry stuff—
The whole thing burned.

KING CANDAULES: Was it all you had, Gyges?

GYGES: No, I had my nets.

They burned up with the cabin.

KING CANDAULES: Can it be! On this same earth,
So close to happiness like mine,
How can such misery be?

Poor Gyges, I should like to see your wife.

ARCHELAUS: So should I.

GYGES: It's easy to have her to see, Candaules. She's not
far away.
Since she's drunk, I was afraid to leave her alone,
So I brought her to the palace with me.

[*Exit* GYGES.]

SEBAS [*nudging* ARCHELAUS, *with a whisper*]:   Archelaus!
We're going to have a good laugh.
She is the one—the wench!

ARCHELAUS [*to* PHARNACES]:   I am aroused myself.
Candaules' idea is really wonderful.
[*To* SEBAS] Is she pretty at least?

SEBAS: Bah! What do you expect of a fisherman's wife?

PHARNACES: Eh! Eh! My dear boy, I have seen peasant
women
Who were not—

196

[*Re-enter* GYGES *with* HIS WIFE; *she looks wild, her hair over her face, badly dressed, drunk.*]

PHÆDRUS: What you are doing, O King, is dangerous.

GYGES [*exposing her*]:   Here you are, gentlemen, the wife
    of Gyges.

ARCHELAUS: Hey! Hey!

KING CANDAULES: Her name?

GYGES: I call her Trydo.

SEBAS: Ah! Ha! If I had known! Trydo! Trydo!

KING CANDAULES: Peace there, gentlemen!

  Let me speak quietly with this man.

  So—poor Gyges, now you have nothing left?

GYGES: For me, it is better to have little

  And be the sole possessor.

SEBAS [*guffaws; then, to* ARCHELAUS]:   Listen to him!

GYGES: Before, I had four things,

  Now I have but two.

  A man can hold two things in hand

  Better than four.

KING CANDAULES: And what are these two, good Gyges?

GYGES: One is my wife.

SEBAS [*bursting out*]:   Ah! Ha! My poor Gyges, you can
    be quite sure

  You are not *her* sole possessor.

KING CANDAULES [*indignant*]:   Sebas!

SEBAS: No! This is too much, this scum

  Coming to play the braggart before me like this,

  Claiming that he alone has touched this woman—

KING CANDAULES: Sebas!

SEBAS: I tell you, while he was out fishing for his yellow
      fish,

[ARCHELAUS *writhes with laughter.*]

   Yesterday, in the kitchen—eh, Trydo?

NYSSIA [*to* CANDAULES]:   My lord, this is frightful. . . .

KING CANDAULES: Sit still, Nyssia.

   I shall not allow this man to be insulted.

GYGES: Thanks, Candaules. And you, sir,

   I do not even know your name

   And care little enough, certainly—

   You have all power over me; I have none over you.

   But I have all over this woman.

   She is mine, I tell you.

[*He takes a knife from the table and stabs her.*]

   She's mine. She's mine. She's mine.

[*Agitation.*]

KING CANDAULES: Stop him.

NICOMEDES: Archelaus! Sebas! Stop him, I say.

[SEBAS, *rising, tangles his feet in his robe and rolls under
the table, dead drunk.* NYSSIA *rises to go out;* NICOMEDES
tries to detain her.]

PHARNACES: Ah, this man is abominable!

KING CANDAULES: No, Pharnaces, he is admirable!

   More a nobleman than you, Sebas. Sebas!

   Where is he?

NICOMEDES: He ran—under the table.

KING CANDAULES: Leave him there, Pharnaces; that is
      where he belongs.

[*Exit* NYSSIA.]

    Nyssia! You are leaving me?

[GYGES *has remained a moment beside his dead wife;
starts to leave.*]

    Stay. Stay, Gyges.

    Gyges!

GYGES: No, Sire.

KING CANDAULES: Gyges!

GYGES: No, I have but one thing, now, on earth.

    No one can take that from me.

KING CANDAULES: What?

GYGES: My poverty.

KING CANDAULES: Yes, Gyges; I am your master;

    I shall take it from you.

GYGES: But I am not your servant, O King.

KING CANDAULES: Well said; do you hear him, Philebus?

       Phædrus?

    No, you are not my servant, brave Gyges!

    And I am not your master,

    But your friend.

    [*To the servants*] Prepare a room for him in the palace.

    Now, gentlemen, up! Surely after so much

    You won't be drinking more. . . .

ACT II

The scene is a room in the palace, open on the left and ending in a sort of terrace where musicians are playing. CANDAULES and GYGES are still at table; before them, the remains of supper. They are stretched out, almost lying down, on low seats. GYGES is gorgeously dressed. The musicians are finishing a symphony.

SCENE I

KING CANDAULES: This music is beginning to annoy me.
   Enough! Gyges has seen what you could do.
   The only exquisite emotion is surprise;
   Our joy is like the water of running streams
   That owes its freshness to its constant flow.
   [*To the musicians*] Go entertain my guests on the ter-
      races.
   Make them my excuses for not appearing this evening,
   I shall stay with Gyges;
   If I join them at all, it will be quite late.
   Go! Let your light music

Keep them from sleep.

[*Exeunt musicians.*]

Clear this table.

[*Servants busy themselves.*]

Leave us the sweetened wine:

Perhaps Gyges will drink more of it. . . .

Offer your cup, Gyges. This wine comes from Cyprus.
Do you like it?

[*To the servants who have cleared the table*]

Now bring in some lamps. Evening is closing in.

Go!

[*Exeunt servants.* CANDAULES *approaches* GYGES.]

My friend Gyges, as you were saying, when the sea was
    cross

You had to go to bed without your supper.

GYGES: Yes, Candaules. More than one poor devil in
    your country

Many an evening goes to bed without his supper.

KING CANDAULES: I wish I had known this before.

GYGES: What's the use?

KING CANDAULES: To trouble myself about it, perhaps.

GYGES: And spoil your happiness?

KING CANDAULES: On the contrary, my happiness would
    have conquered misery. . . .

I thought my happiness was so great, so radiant,

That nothing poor was possible around me.

GYGES: So, you would have done all this for me even
    without knowing me?

KING CANDAULES: Even without knowing you; yes, indeed.

GYGES [*turning away sadly*]:   Do you see, King, friendship is not possible?

KING CANDAULES: But why, O Gyges?

GYGES: It's out of pity you do all this for me.

For a poor man you feel no friendship, you feel pity.

KING CANDAULES: Poor! But you are no longer poor. Get up! Get up!

Look at yourself, Gyges! Your robe has surely changed.

O splendid Gyges, who could pity you now!

[GYGES *rises, looks at his splendid robe, but seems anxious and turns away from* CANDAULES.]

Take this necklace—

[*Unfastens one of his necklaces, tries to put it around* GYGES' *neck.*]

It is my wish.

[GYGES, *wearing the necklace, sits down;* CANDAULES, *insistently, beside him:*]

Do you believe that I am rich?

GYGES: Yes.

KING CANDAULES: Very rich?

GYGES: Very rich, yes.

KING CANDAULES: But tell me—how rich?

GYGES: I know that as far as my sight can reach,

Your kingdom reaches toward the horizon.

KING CANDAULES: O Gyges! It goes far beyond the horizon.

GYGES: They say that you have islands in the sea.

KING CANDAULES: My vessels come back laden from
   them—

   But that is only a meager part of my wealth.

   Can you imagine how much gold is in my cellars?

GYGES: Almost as much as the poor don't have, I imagine.

KING CANDAULES: Do not speak of the poor, Gyges,

   I can make them rich as kings

   And notice no diminution of my fortune.

   Tomorrow we shall visit my palaces.

   Dear Gyges, your cabin was small, wasn't it?

GYGES: Yes, small and cramped, Candaules.

KING CANDAULES: And how many jewels do you think I
   have?

GYGES: You have shown me some beauties.

KING CANDAULES: But I have still finer ones; you will see.

   What is it you used to drink?

GYGES: Water.

KING CANDAULES: Do you like this wine?

GYGES: I am getting used to it.

KING CANDAULES: I have some better.

GYGES [*raising his head from his hands*]:   King Candaules, why are you so anxious

   For me to know about your fortune?

KING CANDAULES: So you may rejoice in our friendship,

   Which makes it possible for you to enjoy this wealth.

GYGES: I thought the friendship you wanted

   Was not for your wealth, but for yourself.

KING CANDAULES: Leave off your irony, Gyges,

And do not resist happiness any longer.

What does it matter that one must give, the other receive,

When two together enjoy the same good?

Listen: anxiety will live in me

So long as you do not know,

In all its complexity all my fortune.

GYGES: King, you possess many things

Whose very name means nothing to me.

What good is it for you to name them

When I cannot even imagine how they taste.

KING CANDAULES: Gyges, I wish to make you taste happiness.

GYGES: A man would better not dream of what he cannot have.

KING CANDAULES: But I shall give you all that, all
that. . . .

Oh, Gyges, Gyges, you were too long unhappy.

Today I wish your pleasure to be greater

Than your pain was great.

[*Servants bring in torches, exeunt. Silence.*]

What is my friend Gyges thinking of? . . .

What were you doing at this same hour last night?

Worn out by the bitter waves,

A lonely fisherman—

GYGES [*interrupting*]:   I was making my way home to
my cabin and Trydo.

KING CANDAULES: Trydo, that's true. Do you miss Trydo?

Poor Gyges! Sit down here beside me.

Tell me. Did you love her?

[GYGES *is still silent.*]

   O Gyges, is your friendship for me
   Without confidence?
   Oh, Gyges, my friend—answer me; tell me.
   Did you love her? Say?

GYGES [*taking his head in his hands, sobbing*]:   On winter nights she was warm in my bed. . . .
   I would say to her: "Trydo"; and she would answer: "Master."
   I believed she loved me, I was happy.

KING CANDAULES: Poor Gyges!

[CANDAULES *rises, restlessly; strides up and down at the back of the hall in disturbed thought; then to himself, in an undertone*]

   What is this you suggest, my unquiet fancy? . . .

[*He puts out several of the torches; then, still standing, turns to* GYGES.]

   Gyges, do you know what first brought me to love you?
   You alone realized the beauty of the Queen. . . .
   Poor Gyges! Before you saw her,
   You thought your wife was beautiful. . . .
   But I saw you suddenly look at Nyssia,
   And all at once Trydo seemed no longer beautiful.

[*Approaching* GYGES]

   Gyges, that is why you killed her, isn't it?

GYGES: O King! How can you think such a thing?

KING CANDAULES: Eh! Am I clever at finding you out?

GYGES: As true as I believe in God, that is not so.

KING CANDAULES [*beginning to pace again*]: Do you believe in God?

GYGES: Certainly, yes.

KING CANDAULES: I don't, very much. You are simple,
You imagine only simple things,
But I—

[*To himself in an undertone*]
Louder, speak louder, my youngest thought!
Where do you mean to lead me? Ah, strange Candau-
les!

[*He paces, extinguishes another torch; then, turning to
GYGES*]
Then, really, it is because—
You were greatly annoyed to know
That your wife did not belong to you alone?

GYGES: That is why I killed her—
Also because I could not kill the other.

KING CANDAULES: Noble Gyges! . . . This is curious—
Does having so few possessions
Make one desire to be their sole possessor?
But—if the other had been your friend?

GYGES: O King, how could a friend think of betraying
me?

KING CANDAULES: Yes—but suppose he had done it without betraying you?

GYGES: I don't understand you, King Candaules.

KING CANDAULES: No matter. . . . So you didn't see the
Queen?

GYGES: Yes, I did, a little; but I didn't look at her.

206

KING CANDAULES: Then you didn't see her.

It's impossible not to look at her if you see her.

[*Lowering his voice*]

She knows it; she doesn't want to be seen again. She
said to me:

"Let this first appearance be my last."

[*Approaching* GYGES, *in a still lower voice*]

Gyges—do you want to see the Queen?

GYGES [*rising, impatiently, pretending not to have heard*]:
I am tired now, let me be.

KING CANDAULES [*holding him back by his robe*]: Gyges
—don't you want to see the Queen?

GYGES [*freeing himself*]: No.

KING CANDAULES: Why?

Gyges, I want to show you Nyssia.

GYGES [*turning to* CANDAULES, *violently*]: I don't want to
see her, at all.

KING CANDAULES [*in a low tone*]: Ah, if you had ever seen
her! . . .

GYGES: So you don't love her?

KING CANDAULES: Oh, more than myself!

So she must not know—

And she loves me so much! . . .

Let me tell you how beautiful she is.

But let me whisper it:

[*Leaning to* GYGES' *ear*]

I have never desired another woman.

Her face is nothing. . . . If you only knew, Gyges!

And her caresses!—If you could only hear her when—

It makes me suffer to hear another woman praised;
I say to myself: it is because they do not know her.
Gyges—do you want to know Nyssia?

GYGES: What! Is all this to test me? I don't understand
   you.

KING CANDAULES: Oh well— Let's turn to other things.
   This necklace that I put about your neck awhile ago,
   All my servants recognize it
   And obey the one who wears it;
   It is the King's necklace; I give it to you.
   Do you still doubt my friendship?

GYGES: Yes—
   So long as you are always the one who gives.
   Let me go now; I am sleepy.

KING CANDAULES [*a little angry*]:   You will sleep later
   on! Stay, Gyges; listen:
   You also have given something—to me.

GYGES: What could it be?

KING CANDAULES: Sit down; come! . . . Stay a little
   longer.

[GYGES *half sits again.*]
   Do you see this ring?
   Even yesterday I set little store by it,
   Because I did not know its value.
   And yet two words engraved under the setting
   Disturbed me as much as its strange origin.
   Gyges, it was buried
   In the flesh of the fish you caught yesterday.
   One of us eating the fish found the ring

And offered it to me; I was surprised and troubled,
And swore not to put it on my finger
Before I had spoken to the fisherman
Whose work had brought this fish to my table.
    Then you came. We talked;
The bloody ending of that dinner
Made me think no longer of the ring.
But, seeing it again this morning—
I was in the company of my noble guests—
And almost without thinking, I put it on my finger.
All at once: "Where has Candaules gone?" said one of
    them.
"Where is he?" "He's gone. He's gone," all said.
And yet I had not budged.
I could see them there
Beside me, as near as I am to you—
But they no longer saw me.
And so, charmed and surprised, full of life and happi-
    ness,
I knew that the ring made me invisible. . . .
I had the courage to say nothing,
And softly slipped away from among them.
My first thought: this ring
I owe to Gyges, to my friend;
I shall show it to him this very evening.
Here it is.

GYGES: Can it be? Am I really your friend, dear Can-
    daules?

KING CANDAULES: Look—watch me closely.

[*With an exaggerated gesture, he puts on the ring.*]

GYGES: Oh! . . . Like a grain·of salt, you are dissolving.

The air is closing upon you—you are gone. Candaules!

Do you still exist? Where are you? . . . Candaules—

[*With another gesture,* CANDAULES *takes off the ring. It is completely useless for* CANDAULES *to be made, by any contrivance whatever, to disappear from the eyes of the audience;* GYGES' *gestures will suffice to indicate that* GYGES *himself no longer sees him. As soon as* CANDAULES *has taken off the ring,* GYGES *throws himself at his feet.*]

Ah, my eyes! . . . Here he is! . . .

You disappear and reappear like a god, King Candaules.

KING CANDAULES: Not like a god, Gyges,

But as you yourself will do

If you will put this ring on your finger. . . .

Here! Put it on.

[GYGES *looks at the ring, fearfully, then dares to slip it on his finger.*]

Oh, a miracle! A dream is not more prompt

To melt from the eyes of a sleeper when he wakes. . . .

Miraculous ring, you also disappear

With the one you cause to disappear;

Now protect the happiness of my friend Gyges, hide
him!

Hide yourself, Gyges! . . . Sh! I hear Nyssia!

[GYGES *moves away, as if terrified; then* CANDAULES, *blindly turning to the spot where he last saw* GYGES, *which is now empty*]

210

KING CANDAULES [*kneeling*]:   Let me—let me take off
    your sandals.

[NYSSIA's *hair comes undone and cascades over* CANDAU-
LES, *kneeling before her.*]

    I love your hair to spill over me.

NYSSIA: That poor fisherman—what became of him?
    Say, won't you answer me? I think you cured him of his
    misery. . . .

KING CANDAULES [*uneasy*]:   Shsh! Hush.

NYSSIA: Why should I hush?
    Do you think I do not know your kindness?

KING CANDAULES: Nyssia!

NYSSIA: What is his name? Tell me.

KING CANDAULES: I do not know.

NYSSIA: The poor man! What he did was terrible!
    But I feel sorry for him.
    Oh, how could a woman—?
    He was right to kill her.
    Belonging to two—oh, it's horrible!

KING CANDAULES: Speak more softly, Nyssia.

NYSSIA: Softly? Why?

KING CANDAULES: These words are painful to me.

NYSSIA: Oh, I am sorry! I will think of it no longer.
    Let's forget that anyone has ever been unfaithful. . . .
    Candaules, my love!

KING CANDAULES: Nyssia, my beloved.

NYSSIA [*finishing her preparations for the night*]:   I can-
    not untie this loop; undo it for me.

[*A faint sound of singing in the distance.*]

Do you hear the singing?

KING CANDAULES: My guests are waiting for me;

They feel it is growing late;

I promised to come back to them this evening.

NYSSIA: Oh, why not forget them, once?

KING CANDAULES [*starting away*]:   For a moment only.

Go to bed, Nyssia,

I shall come back at once. . . . Go to bed, my
sweet. . . . How beautiful you are, Nyssia!

[NYSSIA *is now almost completely undressed.* GYGES, *despite himself, looks on, approaches, obviously struggling, trying not to look; just as* NYSSIA *is about to let fall her last veil, he leaps toward the remaining torch and hurls it to the floor.*]

KING CANDAULES: Gyges!

NYSSIA [*alarmed, pulling bed-curtains or clothes over herself*]:   Oh! What is it?

KING CANDAULES [*exalted and drunk with what he is about to do*]:   Nothing; nothing. Be calm;

I struck the torch in passing. . . .

Go to sleep. Sleep; I shall come back quickly.

[NYSSIA *gets into bed.*]

VOICES OFF STAGE: Candaules! King Candaules! We are
waiting for you; we are weary. . . .

KING CANDAULES [*shouting*]:   I am coming.

[*He stumbles against* GYGES, *who is also trying to leave; the latter is completely maddened, his cloak over his face.* CANDAULES, *in a low voice:*]   It's you, Gyges? Is it you?

GYGES [*very low*]:   Yes, it's me.

216

KING CANDAULES [*imperiously*]:   Stay!
[*Going*]
   And now, all those about me, be happy.
[*Exit.*]

ACT III

The scene is the same as in the first act. SYPHAX, NICOME-
DES, *and* PHARNACES *are in conversation, right.*

SCENE I

SYPHAX: Does this envoy seem to you too much tacked
on?
[*Reading*]
> What do I care for the cupbearer!
> When he pours into my cup
> His clear wine at my shoulder,
> Not to the cupbearer I look up,
> But to Candaules I lift my cup.
> But when Candaules is the cupbearer,
> To the cupbearer I lift my cup up.

NICOMEDES: Yes, your verses are amusing; but I don't
see in what sense
They are addressed to Candaules more than to anyone
else.

PHARNACES: As for me, I don't see how that could possibly bother you.

218

What we praise in a man are the
Virtues that do not belong to him in his own right;
What we love in Candaules is his wealth—
And his generosity, which puts it before us to enjoy.
If he had no generosity, we could not enjoy his wealth.
[*The others protest.*]

    But if he had no wealth, we should not enjoy his gen-
        erosity.
[NICOMEDES *laughs.*]

SYPHAX: And I should not be praising Candaules.

NICOMEDES [*repeating the verses of* SYPHAX]:
          "But when Candaules is the cupbearer,
            To the cupbearer I lift my cup up."
Never mind! If I were a bottle,
I should want to thank Candaules
For letting me give joy to so many men at once.
[PHÆDRUS *and* SIMMIAS *have entered upstage several
moments before; remain somewhat apart from the oth-
ers.*]

PHÆDRUS: If the bottle could talk and should say:
    "I'd rather be sipped by Nicomedes than Candaules,
        because
    He tastes better,"
    Then Candaules would probably be less eager
    To drain it into your glass.

PHARNACES: My dear Phædrus, only bad wine says to
    us:
    "I'd rather be sipped by another."
    Good wine always says, at least to me—

SYPHAX [*interrupting, pulling him by his cloak*]:   Spare
> your wit. Let's go read my verses

Before the banquet— There is only a moment left.

Are you coming, Phædrus, Simmias?

PHÆDRUS: No; your verses will seem better without us;

> You will think you are expressing a more personal senti-
> ment

If only you three express it.

NICOMEDES: I beg your pardon, but I express nothing
> myself; I attend.

PHÆDRUS: We do not attend.

[*The others go off, left;* PHÆDRUS *rejoins* SIMMIAS.]

Let's leave them, Simmias. Our place is not with them.

SIMMIAS: And not in this palace, wouldn't you say,
> Phædrus?

PHÆDRUS: That's true; that's true. Alas, we shall leave.

SIMMIAS: Should we leave Candaules?

PHÆDRUS: I had the keenest affection for him, and es-
> teem;

But since yesterday he is silent, cut off; he seems to
> avoid us.

Ah, Simmias, of what help can our counsel be?

SIMMIAS: But do you mean to leave without seeing him
> again?

PHÆDRUS: No, I am waiting to catch him alone and
> speak to him one last time.

[SEBAS *and* ARCHELAUS *have entered, right; they are ex-
amining the preparations for the banquet.*]

Farewell, Sebas, Archelaus! You must drink, eat, and
enjoy all this.

SEBAS *and* ARCHELAUS: What! You're leaving?

PHÆDRUS: Farewell!

ARCHELAUS: You are making a mistake.

SEBAS: Look, the table is already set for another feast.

PHÆDRUS: When we leave, there will be more for you.
Come, friend.

[*Exeunt* PHÆDRUS *and* SIMMIAS, *left.* SEBAS *and* ARCHE-
LAUS *look at each other, shrug their shoulders.*]

ARCHELAUS: Are you hungry?

SEBAS: Yes.

ARCHELAUS: Already?

SEBAS [*woefully*]:   Archelaus, I am getting fat.

ARCHELAUS: Eat less.

SEBAS: Fie! I might get thin!

ARCHELAUS: But then you could eat more.

SEBAS: Do you think so? My word, you are probably
right.

I shall put this fig back.

Yes, then I can eat more at noon.

[*Enter* PHILEBUS *rapidly, right.*]

PHILEBUS: Have you seen Pharnaces and Syphax?

ARCHELAUS: They were—

SEBAS [*interrupting*]:   Here they are.

[*Re-enter* NICOMEDES, SYPHAX, *and* PHARNACES. PHILEBUS
*is seated on a bench near the banquet table, his hands on
his hips, as if out of breath.*]

221

NICOMEDES: Have you seen Candaules, Philebus? We are looking for him everywhere.

PHILEBUS: I have just left him this instant.

SYPHAX: Well, where is he?

PHILEBUS: Everywhere!

Everywhere and nowhere; he dodges, he prowls, he wanders. . . .

Ah, my friends, do let me laugh!

Ah, what an incredible story! Ha ha!

[*Out of breath from laughing.*]

PHARNACES *and* SEBAS: What do you mean?

PHILEBUS: You know, that ring, which almost choked our Sebas here—

ARCHELAUS: I beg your pardon! It was I who almost choked.

PHILEBUS: All right. It doesn't matter.

ARCHELAUS: But it does matter a good deal to me.

PHILEBUS: Oh well! Just let me tell you.

You remember, Pharnaces,

The Greek words your eyes found written on it?

SEBAS: I beg your pardon! Excuse me! It was Phædrus who saw them.

PHILEBUS: Don't interrupt me.

NICOMEDES, PHARNACES, *and* SYPHAX: Well, go ahead! We are listening.

PHILEBUS: I don't know how it happened, but this evening

The King, though at first he had been disturbed by the two engraved words,

222

Managed to forget the mysterious ring bearing them.

I think the presence of Gyges the fisherman was the
cause.

Ah, my friends, if you knew the rest! It's so funny.

THE OTHERS: Tell us—come on!

PHILEBUS: I don't know how to tell it.

NICOMEDES *and* PHARNACES: Bah! Tell us anyway.

PHILEBUS [*shaken with laughter*]:   No—but if only you
had seen King Candaules!

SYPHAX: Well, what is he doing?

PHILEBUS: He is searching.

SYPHAX *and* PHARNACES: Searching for what?

PHILEBUS [*shouting*]:   The ring.

Listen. Listen—this is the maddest story.

[*All the others are grouped around* PHILEBUS, *who is still
sitting on the bench.*]

Well, it seems that yesterday morning—

Why? I don't know at all;

How? I don't know;

Candaules finally put the ring on his finger.

He was with us. Do you remember, suddenly

We lost sight of him and looked for him?

ARCHELAUS: Yes. Why had he left us?

PHILEBUS: He hadn't left us.

PHARNACES *and* NICOMEDES [*impatient*]:   Go ahead. Explain.

PHILEBUS: It seems that the ring—you won't believe
me.

THE OTHERS: But go ahead, tell us.

You frighten them all, invisible Gyges.
Ring! If you could only hide me from myself!
Gyges is afraid of Gyges.

[*His head in his hands, sobbing*]

Did my harsh embraces hurt you?
I was filled with love and terror; I ran away; I left her
Still asleep, and lying on the edge of the bed . . .
I ran through the night; I fled like a thief,
Over the cold lawn, in the dew to wash away
The fever from my hands, the horror from my mind,
The blushes from my face, the crime from my heart.—
Someone is coming. Where can I hide? It is she!

[*He is still on the floor, leaning against the bench. Enter*
NYSSIA *and* CANDAULES.]

SCENE III

————————

NYSSIA *and* CANDAULES *both sit on the bench.*

NYSSIA [*leaning on* CANDAULES]:   What, my lord! Is that
       the cause of your anxiety?

What was there about this ring, that its loss should
       torment you so?
Was this why you left me so early this morning?
It was hardly dawn; I was still warm, hardly awake;
My hands went seeking you in my bed,
And found, alas, only a cold place.
How could you leave me when I would love you still?

Ah, you do not know what my waking held for
   you! . . .
   Later, when I saw you in the garden,
You were no longer the ardent lover of last night, the
   one I prefer.
   You seem disturbed; what is the matter? Would you
      avoid me?
My lord, I shall be jealous of that ring;
More than your wife it occupies your mind.
Won't you speak to me? Your mouth is ungrateful.
What does this ring matter? You have so many
   riches! . . .
You are always giving, just imagine that you gave it
   away.

KING CANDAULES: Ah, if I could only see it again!

NYSSIA: Meanwhile, chase these wrinkles from your
   brow.
   The morning is so beautiful! See! In the limpid air
   Everything seems in love, as we are, and smiling. . . .
   My lord, I feel almost weary from last night.
   Ah, my lord, your love was more beautiful than the day.
   For me last night was—

KING CANDAULES [*interrupting*]:   Speak no more of last
   night, my dear.

NYSSIA: My lord, I may be silent,
   But your Nyssia remembers it all,
   And still tells your kisses over to herself, one by one.
   Ah, of all our nights, this was the most beautiful night
      of love!

227

KING CANDAULES: Most beautiful, you say, Nyssia—the most beautiful?

NYSSIA: My lord, does it astonish you? What have I said? What is the matter?

KING CANDAULES: The most beautiful—why?

NYSSIA [*blushing*]:   Fie, my lord—you are making light of my emotion . . .

Why are you standing? Are you leaving me? What is the matter?

KING CANDAULES [*aside*]:   You jealous, Candaules? Ah, no, fie!

Evil passion, you will be quiet.

[*He makes a gesture of self-control.*]

I am sorry.

[NYSSIA, *trying to draw him to the bench, grasps a fold of his robe.*]

No, let me alone.

[*He frees himself; aside*]

The most beautiful! . . . Ah, at least I should like to know why. . . .

I must see Gyges again, absolutely.

[*He has moved away, left; to* NYSSIA]

I see Phædrus yonder.

Excuse me, I'll be back in a moment.

No, don't follow me. Let me go, Nyssia.

NYSSIA: Then I shall wait for you here. Come back quickly.

[*During this scene* GYGES *has quietly risen.*]

SCENE IV

GYGES [*in an undertone*]:   The most beautiful of nights!
. . . Enough, ring! Enough!
[*Snatches the ring from his finger.*]
Even if I die for it, I must speak to her!
[*He straightens his disordered clothes, approaches her.*]
Madam!
NYSSIA [*surprised, lowering her veil*]: Ah! You star-
tled me!
I heard no one approaching.
GYGES [*bowing*]: Ah, madam—
NYSSIA: What do you want?
GYGES [*offering her the ring*]:   Here is the ring—the one
Candaules is seeking.
NYSSIA: If you knew he was searching for it,
Why didn't you return it to him at once?
GYGES: I wish to return it first to you.
NYSSIA: But how is it that you have this ring?
GYGES: The King gave it to me.
NYSSIA: If he gave it to you, why is he looking for it?
GYGES: Not to have the ring back, but to see me again.
NYSSIA: I do not understand you. But who are you?
You were not at the banquet, I believe, the other eve-
ning.
GYGES: Oh yes—but I did not arrive until the end.
I am Gyges. Do you remember, madam,

Gyges, the fisherman you asked about
Last night, when you said to Candaules:
"What became of that poor fisherman?"
Here he is.

NYSSIA [*a little disconcerted*]:   How could I recognize
   you in those fine clothes, fisherman?
The King's kindness gave you all this?

GYGES [*embarrassed*]:   Yes, Queen; he gave me all this
   —all this—
And this ring.

[*Bows again, offering it to her.*]

NYSSIA: I shall give it back to him.

GYGES: I beg you—one word more, madam—this ring—

[*The* QUEEN *looks at the ring, is about to put it on her
   finger.*]

Ah, do not put it on your finger!

NYSSIA: Why?

GYGES [*uneasy for what he is about to say*]:   This ring—

NYSSIA: Speak, fisherman.

GYGES: Makes whoever wears it—invisible.

NYSSIA [*smiling*]:   Certainly, then, it is a very precious
   ring. I understand
Now why Candaules was so anxious to find it.

GYGES: Also, perhaps, why he was unable to find it.

NYSSIA [*beginning to feel uneasy*]:   Were you hiding,
   Gyges?

GYGES: It was hiding me, madam.

NYSSIA: But tell me—why did the King give you this
   ring?

230

GYGES: So that I might see without being seen.

NYSSIA: And what could the King
  Possibly wish you to see?

GYGES [*falling to his knees at her feet*]: You, Nyssia!

[*He suddenly hands her a dagger; she takes it instinctively.*]

  Strike me! Strike me! Last night it was I—
  I left you this morning asleep. . . .
  Ah, I could have kept silent, you would never have
    known,
  But I was also here just now when you said
  That last night was of all nights of love—

NYSSIA [*only beginning to understand, her shame and
  horror increasing at every word, interrupts him
  with a cry*]: Candaules!—Horror! Horror! I
  thought—I was loved!

GYGES [*straightening up*]: But you were, madam. . . .

NYSSIA [*furious*]: What are you saying?

GYGES [*tenderly*]: You are, Nyssia.

NYSSIA [*suddenly making up her mind, puts the dagger
  in his hand*]: Go stab him.

GYGES [*wildly*]: Who?—Him?

NYSSIA: Go stab him.

GYGES [*dropping the dagger*]: No! He is—
  My friend!

NYSSIA: Yes, and he was my husband! Kill him.

GYGES: I cannot. He gave me—

NYSSIA: He betrayed me.

[*Tearing her veil from her face*]

231

He is coming. One of you must die.

Quickly—take the ring. Stab him! Stab him!

GYGES [*desperate*]:   When he cannot see me?

NYSSIA: You were hidden from me!

GYGES: He gave me the ring.

NYSSIA [*exasperated by his resistance*]:   At least one of
    you has to be jealous!

[*She seizes* GYGES *and kisses him violently on the lips.*]

Oh, you will strike him, Gyges. You will stab him!

The ring! Put on the ring.

[*She puts it on his finger.*]

Now hide! Here he is.

[*Enter* CANDAULES *with* PHÆDRUS, *in conversation;* NYSSIA
and GYGES *withdraw to the back of the stage.*]

SCENE V

———————

KING CANDAULES [*to* PHÆDRUS, *in a low voice*]:   No,
    Phædrus, if you love me

Stay awhile, until the banquet;

This is the last, I tell you; the last. . . .

They will not have finished drinking

Before I say: "Now, leave me;

This palace, these festive meals

Must now be shared by me alone,

With Nyssia."

Nyssia, I tell you: I shall close her round
Now, in the dark, away from all, for myself alone;
Like a subtle perfume, that might evaporate. . . .
No more, let's speak no more of her at the moment;
    here she is.
You will be at the banquet?

PHÆDRUS: I shall.

KING CANDAULES: Leave me, then.

[*Exit* PHÆDRUS. *To* NYSSIA]

The banquet is set . . . It is nearly noon,
The hour when my noble guests will come.
Nyssia, let me see you to your chamber.

[*He approaches her, she draws back.* GYGES *is somewhat behind them.*]

NYSSIA: No. I am coming to the banquet.

KING CANDAULES: What? You wish—?

[*Noticing the* QUEEN's *troubled state*]

What is the matter, Nyssia?

NYSSIA [*still drawing back, then speaking into vacancy*]:
    Strike! Strike! Gyges! Take care, Candaules.

[*Anxiously*] Stab him! Ah! Go on, strike! . . .

[GYGES *stabs* CANDAULES *just as the latter begins to feel uneasy.*]

KING CANDAULES [*falling to the floor, left*]:   What! It's
    you, my own Gyges?
Why did you strike me?
I felt nothing in me but kindness.
Nyssia! . . . Gyges, I gave you the knife too.

Take off your ring—

I want to see you again.

[GYGES *hesitates a moment, then throws the ring away.*]

GYGES [*terrified and grieved, kneels to* CANDAULES, *leaning toward him*]:   Candaules, my friend—

[CANDAULES *dies.*]

NYSSIA [*pulling at* GYGES' *robe*]:   Stand up! King Gyges!

GYGES [*haggard*]:   Me! Gyges!—King!

NYSSIA: You are my husband; I am the Queen.

These are your guests. Stand up! Compose yourself!

[*She lifts the diadem from* CANDAULES' *turban.*]

Put on this crown.—Ah, this veil stifles me.

[*She snatches it completely off.*]

NOBLES [*approaching; a stir*]:   Candaules!

Oh!

How horrible!

SYPHAX [*detaining* PHÆDRUS *and pointing to* GYGES]:
        Shsh. Be careful! . . .

NYSSIA [*regally, on* GYGES' *arm*]:   Dear lords, are you
        coming? The banquet awaits you.

Archelaus! This evening there will be dancing girls.

[*Exit* PHÆDRUS, *taking* SIMMIAS.]

GYGES [*gradually recovering*]:   Be seated, gentlemen.

[*Hostilely, to* NYSSIA]

I thought so beautiful a face, madam,

Should be veiled.

NYSSIA [*contemptuously*]:   Veiled for you, Gyges. Candaules tore away my veil.

234

GYGES [*brutally covering her face with part of her garment*]:   Well, sew it on again.

SYPHAX [*in the midst of the stir provoked by this gesture*]:
Come, gentlemen, let us drink to Gyges' happiness!

END

❈

Persephone

AN OPERA IN THREE SCENES

1933

TO MME IDA RUBINSTEIN

*whose fervor revived an idea that had been
asleep for twenty years*

CHARACTERS

PERSEPHONE

EUMOLPE

MERCURY

DEMETER

TRIPTOLEMUS

SPIRIT OF DEATH

CHORUS OF NYMPHS

CHORUS OF SHADES

CHORUS OF DANAÏDES

CHORUS OF YOUTHS

PROCESSION OF HOURS

SCENE I

EUMOLPE [*front stage, before the curtain*]:   Goddess of
  a thousand names, O great
  Demeter, thou coverest
  The earth with harvest,
  Thou dispenser of wheat;
  Here before these assembled people,
  Thy mysteries let us celebrate.

[*The curtain rises on a seaside meadow; on the right, a slope of grass and flowers, among which the large narcissus blooms; on the left, a rocky pass leading to Hell, where* PERSEPHONE *is to go down.*]

  Now unto the Nymphs thou dost
  Thy dear Persephone entrust,
  Thy daughter. Only she can bring
  Flowers to earth, and make it Spring.
  How she was stolen from you,
  Homer tells the story.

[*Forewarned by* MERCURY, *who is taking* PERSEPHONE *away,* DEMETER *bids her farewell and commends her to the* NYMPHS.]

CHORUS OF NYMPHS: Stay with us, Persephone, princess,
  Thy mother Demeter, queen of summer,
  Left you in our care,
  Among the birds and flowers,
  The kissing streams, and the caressing air;

239

See, on the wave, the sun laughing!

Stay, in all this happiness.

It is the world's first morning.

PERSEPHONE [*still sitting, as if half asleep*]:   The wayward breezes

Fondle the flowers.

[CHORUS OF NYMPHS *gathers around* PERSEPHONE, *who is
slowly rising.*]

CHORUS OF NYMPHS: Come! Play with us, dear daughter. . . .

The breezes fondle the flowers,

It is the world's first morning;

Things are as glad as our hearts,

Laughing on land and water.

Come! Play with us, dear daughter:

The breezes fondle the flowers.

PERSEPHONE [*spoken part*]:   I hear you with all my heart,

Song of the world's first morning.

CHORUS OF NYMPHS: Delight of morning,

New light, and petals

Streaming with juices.

Wait not, surrender

Now to the tender

Word, let the future

Sweetly invade you

With tender uses.

PERSEPHONE [*spoken part*]:   So subtle now becomes

The tepid kiss of day,

The timidest soul to love

Would give itself away.

CHORUS OF NYMPHS: Hyacinth, verbena,

Columbine and crocus,

Pheasant's-eye narcissus,

And all the flowers of Spring . . .

EUMOLPE: Of all the flowers of Spring

The loveliest is the narcissus.

Whoever stoops to its cup

To drink in its sweet smell

Shall see the unknown world of Hell.

[*The* CHORUS *moves in a dance designed to keep* PERSEPH-
ONE *from coming near the narcissus.* PERSEPHONE *breaks
the circle of* NYMPHS, *approaches, and stoops over the
flower.*]

CHORUS OF NYMPHS: Beware, be on your guard.

Let not yourself, with hollow

Eyes and features, follow

What you love too hard.

Come not near the narcissus.

No, gather not this flower!

EUMOLPE: Whoever stoops to its cup

To drink in its sweet smell

Shall see the unknown world of Hell.

PERSEPHONE [*stooping over the flower*]:   I see meadows
        starred with asphodel

And shadows slowly drifting.

On they go, plaintive and faithful,

Drifting shades they are,

A whole hopeless people,

Sad, unquiet, and colorless.

[*The* CHORUS *surrounds* PERSEPHONE, *watching and leaning anxiously toward her. A new anxiety begins to be
heard in the orchestra which up to now has been ex-
pressing pure joy.*

The CHORUS *tries, despite the anxiety in the orchestra,
to recover its joy, and sweep* PERSEPHONE *with it.*]

CHORUS OF NYMPHS: Gather not this flower, Persephone.
Let not yourself, with hollow
Eyes and features, follow
What you love too hard.
Come! Play with us, Persephone.

[*A great wail runs through the orchestra.* PERSEPHONE
*has plucked the flower. Her dance expresses anxiety and
grief. She comes down slowly from the grassy knoll where
the narcissus grew, and goes toward the rocks on the left.*

The NYMPHS *try to restrain her, but she moves ahead
as if enthralled, her eyes fixed on the narcissus which she
holds in her hand.* PERSEPHONE'S *entire role is spoken,
not sung.*]

EUMOLPE: Persephone, your people
Await you, a doleful people
Who know no hope, who never
Can see the Spring smile.
Persephone, your people
Await you, for already
Your pity has betrothed you
To Pluto, King of Hell.

You must go down to him and console the shades,
Your youth will make their grief less dark, your Spring
On their eternal Winter will cast its spell.
Come! You shall be queen of the shades.

PERSEPHONE: Nymphs, my sisters, charming friends,
How could I henceforth
Lightly laugh and sing with you,
Now that I have seen, now that I know
An unrequited people is waiting,
Living in suffering. O sorrowing
People of shadow,
I am drawn to you. I shall go. . . .

SCENE II

The stage is now dark. Continuous music. Curtain.

EUMOLPE: And so it was, as told by Homer,
That Pluto, Hell and Winter's king,
Stole Persephone from her mother,
And from the earth, Spring.

[*The curtain rises. The scene is the Elysian Fields. On the right, the door to Pluto's palace.* PERSEPHONE *lying on a bed of state, beneath a dais supported by columns. Near her, still asleep, the* CHORUS OF SHADES. *On the left, the banks of the river overhung with the boughs of an immense tree. Beside the river, the* CHORUS OF DANAÏDES,

243

*dressed in ashen green, are ceaselessly drawing water
from the river, inclining their urns one toward another.
The background is obscured by clouds.*]

CHORUS: On her bed there
  She reposes
  And I dare
  Not disturb her. She still dozes
  Half awake, and presses to her heart
  The narcissus bloom
  Whose perfume
  Made her pity start.

PERSEPHONE [*reclining*]:   In what strange place am I
        waking . . . where am I,
  Is it evening already? Or near the end of night?

CHORUS: Nothing here can end,
  Here each one pursues,
  Endlessly pursues
  What flows away to no end. . . .

EUMOLPE: Here the death of time makes life eternal.

PERSEPHONE: What am I doing here? . . .

EUMOLPE: You are Queen of the Shades.

PERSEPHONE: O plaintive Shades, what are you doing?

CHORUS OF DANAÏDES: We watch ever
  By the river
  Of eternity
  By the very
  Shallow water
  Of the river Lethe.
  Each in turn

With her urn
At the silent river
Draws in vain
From a fountain
That flows away forever.

PERSEPHONE: Rest now, sorrowful Shades.

CHORUS:
[*Repeats:* "Nothing here can end," *etc.*]

PERSEPHONE: What can I do to make you happy?

CHORUS OF DANAÏDES: We are not unhappy.
No hate, no envy,
No love, and no pain.
We have no destiny
But again and again
To make the meaningless gesture
Of life.

CHORUS OF SHADES: Tell us of Spring, immortal Persephone.

PERSEPHONE: Mother Demeter, how beautiful the earth
Was when our loving laughter brought to birth
Flowers among the golden wheat, in milk
Its fragrance. Now I am far from thee, and lost!
And endlessly throughout the unending day
Pale flowers appear, on which my eyes repose. . . .
On the gray banks of Lethe blooms the white rose
And in the shade of evening's uncertain glimmer,
Charms the dead shades with subterranean summer.

CHORUS: O speak to us, immortal Persephone.

[*Silence in the orchestra.*]

PERSEPHONE [*nearly speechless*]:   Who is calling to me?

EUMOLPE: Pluto!

You have come here to rule,
Not to pity, Persephone.
Do not hope to be helpful.
None, not even God, escapes from Destiny.
Yours is to be queen. Accept it.
And to forget your pity
Drink this cup of Lethe,
The gift of Hell.
With it come all earth's treasures.

[SHADES, *draped in black, come from Pluto's palace laden with jewels and ornaments; one holding a cup gives it to the last of the* DANAÏDES, *who fills it with water of Lethe. The* SHADE *then approaches* PERSEPHONE.]

PERSEPHONE [*takes the jewels, looks at them sadly, rejects them*]:   No, take these jewels away.

The frailest meadow flower
Is better ornament.

EUMOLPE: Come, Mercury!

Come, Hours of day and night.

[*High upstage, back, the clouds open and* MERCURY *leaps out, followed by the procession of* HOURS. MERCURY'S *role is silent. The* HOURS *are dressed in light colors, graduated in tones of dawn, daybreak, daylight, etc. Each bears a gift for* PERSEPHONE.]

Persephone, bemused,
Has refused
All that should be her delight.

246

Yet Mercury
Hopes that in her mother's memory
A fruit may tempt her sight,
A fruit that first
He sees upon the bough
Bending now
Above the fatal thirst
Of Tantalus.
He plucks the ripe pomegranate
Looking to make sure
That some pure
Sunshine is left upon it,
Offers it to Persephone,
Who marvels, astonished
To find here in her night
A reminder of earth's light,
The lovely color of delight.
Now with more confidence
She smiles,
Gives way to her appetite,
Seizes the pomegranate,
Takes a bite. . . .
At once
Mercury flies off and
Pluto smiles.

[*Music in quick rhythm; strident and ironical when*
MERCURY, *in* EUMOLPE'S *song, leaps up to seize the pome-*
granate. He offers it to PERSEPHONE. *She hesitates, then*
takes it, and bites. With EUMOLPE'S *last words,* MERCURY

247

and the procession of Hours *are gone. Only* Persephone
and the Chorus of Shades *remain.*]

persephone: Where am I? . . . What have I done?
        . . . What troubles me?
   Sustain me, sisters! Ah, the taste of fruit
   Has given me back the taste of my lost earth.
chorus: If you would gaze
   On the narcissus flower
   It might awaken
   Again in you the power
   To see your forsaken
   Meadows and your mother,
   As once to you on earth
   The mystery
   Of the lower world appeared.
persephone: Come close around me, guard me, faithful
        Shadows.
   This flower, the most beautiful in the meadows,
   Is all the Spring that I could bring to Hell.
   If I should lean down to it, question it,
   What could it show me? . . .
eumolpe: Winter.

[Persephone, *surrounded by the* Chorus of Shades,
*front stage, takes the narcissus flower from her girdle,
gazes at it.*]

persephone: Where have you fled, O fragrances and
        songs,
   Escorts of love? . . . All that I see is dead.
   The flowerless meadows and the cropless fields

Tell but their longing for a brighter season.
On all the hillsides the bucolic flute
That filled the woods with music now is mute.
And a long moan flows from everything,
For all is vainly longing for the Spring.
Come, add to mine, in turn, your sorrowful voice.

CHORUS: What do you see?

PERSEPHONE: . . . Rivers locked in ice;
  Streams that used to run away in tears
  Now hushed in frost. Through a dark wood, at night,
  I see my mother wandering in rags,
  Begging the world for lost Persephone.
  Alone, through thickets, over trackless land,
  Walking, walking, with a torch in her hand.
  O thorns, winds, stones, O branches gnarled and coarse,
  Why do you tear her in her painful course?
  Mother, seek no more. Thy daughter lives
  In Hell, and sees, but is no more for thee.
  Alas—if only my bewildered words
  Could—

CHORUS: No, Demeter will hear your voice
  No more, Persephone. . . .

EUMOLPE: But Winter cannot be eternal,
  Poor desperate Shades.

[*From this point the music begins the long crescendo, or
rather the ascent toward clarity, which is to continue to
the end of this scene and introduce the joyous solemnity
of the next.*]

  Demeter has come

To the palace of Eleusis
Where King Seleucus
Has given to her care
His last-born child
Demophoön,
Triptolemus to be.

PERSEPHONE: A cradle of burning sticks and flame I see.
I see Demeter stooping over him.

EUMOLPE: Wouldst thou take him from human destiny,
Goddess? Of a mortal make a god?
For food and drink thou givest him
Not milk, but nectar and ambrosia.
The child smiles toward life and prospers.

CHORUS: And hope is born again in our charmed spirits.

PERSEPHONE: I see my mother walking on the shore,
Holding in her arms the happy child
And rocking him in cadence with the waves.
Touching his nostrils with the moistened air
She gives him, naked, to the salty breeze.
How beautiful! Radiant with sun and health
He leaps, and runs to immortality.
Hail, Demophoön, the one hope of my heart!
Shall I, through you, look on the earth again
In flower? You must teach mankind to till
The fields, as Mother once taught you.

EUMOLPE: Your labor shall bring back Persephone
To love, to light, to life.

PERSEPHONE: Shall I escape the dreaded lower world?
Shall meadows smile with me? Shall I be queen?

CHORUS: Of Spring on earth, no longer Queen of Hell.

PERSEPHONE: Thou dost await me, Demeter, thy arms
    Are wide to take thy daughter being born
    Again to the full sun and pleasant shadows.
    Come! Come, and let us force the doors of death.
    No, dreadful Pluto cannot hold us back.
    Soon we shall see the branches of the trees
    Delicately swaying in the breeze.
    O earthly mate, I hear you call above,
    I come, shining Triptolemus, my love!

[PERSEPHONE *is directed toward the back of the stage,
which lights up, while the front of the stage darkens.*]

CURTAIN

SCENE III

EUMOLPE [*during the scene change*]:   Let us see now,
        as in Homer,
    How Demophoön's labors bring
    Persephone unto her mother,
    And unto the earth, Spring!

[*Upstage, a hill on which stands a Doric temple. Downstage, left, a tumulus covered with evergreen oaks, on one
side of which, at an angle to the audience, is the door of
a tomb, closed with heavy stone panels, like an Etruscan
tomb. Before this funeral porch stands the* SPIRIT OF
DEATH, *with an extinguished torch in his hand.*]

    On this hill rising

251

Above present and future
The Greeks have built a temple
To Demeter,
And she looks down
On a happy people
Coming up from the town.
Triptolemus is beside her
With his gleaming sickle,
And the faithful
Chorus of Nymphs come after.

[*A* CHORUS OF YOUTHS *approach to join the* CHORUS OF NYMPHS.]

CHORUS OF NYMPHS: Come join us, sons of men.

CHORUS OF YOUTHS: Receive us, daughters of the gods.

DOUBLE CHORUS: Here we bring
  Our offering:
  Garlands
  Of lilies, buttercups, cornflowers,
  Saffron, crocus, and anemone . . .
  Flowers for Persephone;
  For Demeter, grain.
  The wheat is yet green
  But the rye is yellow.

CHORUS OF YOUTHS: Queen of Summer, Demeter,
  Give us of thy serenity.

CHORUS OF NYMPHS: Come back to us, Persephone,
  Burst the doors of the tomb!
  Relight your lamp, and come,
  Archangel of death.

Demeter awaits you. Triptolemus
Strips off her mantle of mourning
That still covers her,
And scatters the grave with flowers.

DOUBLE CHORUS: Open, fatal doors,
Dead lamp, extinguished flame,
Revive and live. It is time.
Time for you to come
From the abyss of night, dear Spring.

[*The stone portals roll on their hinges.* PERSEPHONE *arises from the tomb.*]

EUMOLPE: Still heavy, her eyes
Are glad with surprise
As Persephone steps
From the sinister room.
Hesitant, dazed
With night, from the grave,
Hardly believing
That you are living,
Yet you do live.

CHORUS OF YOUTHS: Staggering maid,
Still covered with shade
As if caught in a net,
Wherever your foot
In tentative pose
On the earth is set,
That moment is heard
A singing bird.
There springs a rose.

Your gesture sets free
The language of dance,
Saying joy, confidence,
And light, all three
Are found in a flower.
All nature leaves night
And drinks the fresh light.
You—leap toward the day.

CHORUS OF NYMPHS: But why are you silent,
  So grave and quiet,
  When love awaits?

[PERSEPHONE *has joined* DEMETER, TRIPTOLEMUS, *and the*
CHORUS OF NYMPHS *on top of the hill, near the temple.
Mystic rites of betrothal.*]

CHORUS OF YOUTHS: What does Winter hide that we
        should know?
  Speak, Persephone, and tell.

[*Silence in the orchestra.*]

CHORUS OF NYMPHS: With you, what secrets from below
  Up from those chasms well?

DOUBLE CHORUS: Tell us what you saw in Hell?

PERSEPHONE: Mother, thy Persephone has come.
  Thy robe of mourning, stained with Winter's darkness,
  Shines again with flowers and new splendor.
  And you, my sister Nymphs, your faithful troupe
  Are footing new grass now in the green thicket.
  And you, Triptolemus, my earthly mate,
  Tiller of earth, the fertile grain you sow
  Already sprouts and grows to fecund harvest. . . .

You cannot halt the progress of the seasons.
Night succeeds to day, winter to fall.
Take me, I am your own Persephone,
But I am wife as well to somber Pluto.
No, you can never with so strong a hold
Lock me in your arms, Demophoön,
But that I may escape the embrace and go,
Despite my love for you, my breaking heart,
To answer destiny. For I must go
Down to the shadowy world of suffering.
Do not imagine a heart drunk with love
Can once stoop down to Hell's abyss of sorrows
And ever again go free. For I have seen
Things that are hidden, that avoid the light.
Never can I forget you, sorrowful truth.
Here is Mercury, who with my consent
Will take me; for without command I go
Freely now where love, not law, must lead.
Slowly, step by step, I shall go down,
Down to the bottom of human misery.

[PERSEPHONE *takes the lighted torch from the hands of* MERCURY. *Then, led by* MERCURY, *she goes slowly and solemnly down to the door of the tomb, which opens before her. The* NYMPHS *surround* DEMETER *and* TRIPTOLEMUS. EUMOLPE *and the* CHORUS OF YOUTHS *remain on the hillside.*]

EUMOLPE: Down to the dark below
    You slowly make your way
    Bearing a torch, O queen

255

Of the vast lands of sleep.
You carry to the shades
A little light of day,
Relief for their many woes,
A little love for their sorrows.

For Spring to be reborn
The seed must consent to go
Under ground and die
So it may come up again
The future's golden grain.

END

The Evolution

of the

Theater

TO EMILE VERHAEREN

A LECTURE DELIVERED AT THE
Société de la Libre Esthétique,
BRUSSELS, MARCH 25, 1904.

LADIES AND GENTLEMEN:

THE evolution of the art of drama is a particularly difficult subject. I should like to begin by telling you why. Perhaps you will then allow me to talk rather than to lecture, and to talk around the subject rather than on the subject itself.

Since I consider that dramatic works do not find, nor mean to find, their aim and end in themselves (and this makes for one of the worst difficulties of the subject), but that the dramatist sets his work up, so to speak, between the audience and the actor, I propose to take, in succession, first the author's, then the actor's, and then the spectator's point of view, in an effort to consider, each in turn, these three aspects of one and the same evolution.

Another difficulty, not among the least, comes from the fact that in the success of a play, or even of a whole genre of plays, many considerations may be involved which have nothing to do with literature. I speak not only of the manifold elements that dramatic works must draw on in order to be successfully performed: the wealth of scenery, brilliant costumes, beautiful women, the talent and celebrity of actors; I speak especially of certain preoccupations, social, patriotic, pornographic, or pseudo-artistic, of the author.

The successful plays of today are often tissues of just these preoccupations; so much so that by dropping them one at a time we almost annihilate the play.[1]

But for the most part it is precisely to these preoccupations that the play owes its popularity; the author who does not give in to them, but who writes solely out of a preoccupation with art, is quite likely not even to see his work performed.

Now, since dramatic works live only potentially in books, live completely only on the stage, the critic who today would take an interest in the evolution of the theater would be obliged, in order not to neglect the parallel evolution of actor and audience, to speak of works that have only a very distant relation to literature, and on the other hand to neglect plays of purely literary

[1] The same preoccupations exist, it is true, for the novel also; but besides the fact that they are a great deal less harmful to it because the novel is a vague, multiform, and omnivorous literary species, the novelist who allows himself to be guided by them turns his back on literature in a franker fashion. And however bumptious the publicity that may precede or follow it, a bad book, written to be sold, is not, after all, presented in a much more impertinent manner than a good one. Better still: boosting puts us on guard; when a writer like Champsaur announces that his *Arriviste*, even before publication, has reached its . . . 30th thousand, the public knows what to think, of book and author alike. We are never taken in by novels as we are by works in the theater; the playwright, moreover, is never alone involved; there are also the actors, the producer, and his expenses. A serious literary critic never mentions, never even reads, books of the mediocrity of many plays to which our leading dramatic critics think they are obliged to devote several columns.

merit; here I refer not only to works like Francis Viélé-Griffin's *Phocas*, Henri de Régnier's *La Gardienne*, or Francis Jammes's *Un Jour*, which I agree may be considered as poems only, but to the early plays of Maeterlinck, the dramas of Claudel, Henri Ghéon's *Le Pain*, and others (I was about to say *Le Cloître* of Verhaeren, but remembered the happy success it has won in Brussels and elsewhere). Or if our critic does speak of these works, it can only be as events in the world of books, unknown to the stage and to the theater audience; their evolution not only remains apart from the other, quite apart, but even runs counter to it.

"In social animals," writes Darwin, natural selection "will adapt the structure of each individual for the benefit of the whole community; if the community," he adds, "profits by the selected change." Here the community does not profit; it does not wish to profit. The artist whose work is not performed buries himself in his work, escapes the general evolution, and ends by reacting against it. The works of which I speak are all works of reaction.

Reaction against what? I should readily say against realism, were it not that the word *realism*, which has already been given so many different senses, would quickly prove a serious handicap to me as well. The cleverest hypocrisy I could use would not suffice to convict the works of Monsieur Rostand, for example, of realism, nor the comedies of Molière nor the dramas of Ibsen of anti-realism. Let us say, rather, a reaction against episodism. Yes, for the lack of a better, *episodism* seems to me the preferable word. For art does not consist in the use of heroic, historical, or legendary figures; nor is it necessarily inartistic to put contemporary bourgeois figures on the stage. Yet there is some truth in Racine's words, which I read from the preface to *Bajazet:* "Characters in tragedy must be regarded with a different eye than we ordinarily regard those persons we have seen close to. It may be said," he adds, "that the respect we have for heroes increases as they are farther from us." It may be said, however, I venture to add in turn, that respect for characters on the stage is perhaps not indispensable. The artist chooses figures distant from us for the reason that time, or any kind of distance, allows an image to reach us only after it has been stripped of everything episodic, bizarre, and transitory, leaving only its portion of profound truth for art to work on. And the sense of strangeness that the artist seeks to produce by putting his characters at a distance from us indicates just this desire: to give us his work of art as a work of art, his drama as drama simply, and not to run after an illusion of reality which, even if it were attained, would only serve to form upon reality a pleonasm. Was it not this very desire that urged our classical writers, almost without their knowledge, to be bound by the three unities: to make drama deliberately and plainly artistic.

Whenever art languishes we order it back to nature, as we take a sick person to a watering-place. This is a mistake: nature, alas, cannot help. I agree that it may be good sometimes for art to go to the country; if it is pale from exhaustion, that it go to the fields,—that is, to life— to regain its strength. But our masters, the Greeks, knew well enough that Aphrodite was not born of any natural fecundation. Beauty will never be produced by natural means; it can only be obtained by artificial constraint. Art and nature are rivals on earth. Yes, art embraces nature, and holds it; but citing the celebrated line, art might well say:

"*J'embrasse mon rival; mais c'est pour l'étouffer.*" [2]

Art is always the result of constraint. To believe that it rises higher as it becomes freer is to believe that what keeps a kite from rising is its string. Kant's dove, which thought it could fly better without the air to trouble its wings, did not realize that in order to fly, it had to have the air's resistance to support its wings. Likewise art must be supported by resistance in order to rise. I have mentioned the three dramatic unities, but what I am saying at present is quite as true also for painting, sculpture, music, and poetry. Art aspires to freedom only in periods of illness, when it would prefer to live easily. Whenever it feels vigorous, it seeks struggle and obstacle. It loves to burst out of its sheath, and for that reason it prefers a tight one. Is it not in periods when life is most overflowing that the need of the strictest forms torments our most moving geniuses? Hence the use of the sonnet during the luxuriant Renaissance, by Shakespeare, Ronsard, Petrarch, and even Michelangelo; hence Dante's use of

[2] I embrace my rival, but only to choke him.

terza rima; Bach's love of the fugue; and the restless need of the constraint of the fugue in the later works of Beethoven. How many more examples could be cited! Should we be astonished that the lyrical impulse's power of expansion is due to its compression; or that the weight to be supported is what makes architecture possible?

The great artist is one who is exalted by his difficulties, who uses an obstacle as a springboard. It has been said that Michelangelo owed to the very flaw in the marble his creation of the compact movement of his Moses. It was the limited number of speakers at his disposal on the stage that constrained Æschylus to imagine the silence of Prometheus being chained to the rock in the Caucasus. Greece banished the man who added a string to the lyre. Art is born of constraint, lives by struggle, dies of freedom.

The dramatist little by little diminished the space that separates the stage from the audience, boasting at first that he was gaining for drama in power of expression what it lost at once in beauty. It seems that this evolution was fated; the actor also did his best to diminish that "distance" which Racine required between the spectator and the figure on the stage, and to humanize the hero. He threw away, in turn, mask and buskin—in short, everything that made of him something strange, to be regarded, if I may repeat Racine's words, "with a different eye than we ordinarily regard those persons we have seen close to." He did away even with the conventional costume which, by taking the dramatic character out of its historical period, by abstracting him so to speak, allowed only that precisely to remain which was general and human. If there was any progress in that, it was at least very dangerous progress. Under the pretext of truth, the actor sought accuracy. Costumes, properties, scenery, all did their best to identify exactly the place and time of the action, with never a care that Racine, for example, had taken care to do the opposite. We read in Goethe: "There are, properly speaking, no historical figures in poetry; only, when the poet wishes to portray the world that he has conceived, he chooses certain persons he has met with in history and does them the honor of borrowing their names and applying them to the beings of his own crea-tion." [3] I have taken these lines just as they are quoted by Victor Hugo in one of the notes to his *Cromwell:* "One is astonished," he says, "to read these lines from Herr Goethe." Today we are perhaps less astonished.

But on this point the dramatist has the actor against him. Talma, when he was supposed to play the *Mahomet* of Voltaire, thought it well to study the Mahomet of his-tory first, for a whole month. He himself relates how, "having found too many and too great discrepancies be-tween the one he had conceived and the one Voltaire presented, he had immediately renounced the role be-cause it would have been impossible for him to render it without departing from the truth." I quote from the text of Guiraud's memoirs; I could not have invented a better

[3] *Über Kunst und Alterthum.*

constrain himself to be commonplace, but drove himself to excel by virtue; each man exacted of himself only what was in him, and without deformation modeled himself on his god. Hence the great number of gods, as numerous as the instincts of men. It was not by free choice that man devoted himself to a particular god; the god recognized his own image in the man. Sometimes it happened that the man refused to see it; and the god unrecognized in the man took vengeance; this happens most terribly to Pentheus in the *Bacchantes* of Euripides.

Pagans rarely considered qualities of the soul as goods that could be acquired, but rather as natural properties like those of the body. Agathocles was good, or Charicles courageous, quite as naturally as one had blue eyes, the other black. For them religion did not hold up on a cross, or set up before them on earth, any bundle of virtues or any moral phantom that it was important to resemble, under pain of being considered ungodly; the typical man was not one, but legion; or rather there was no typical man. In those days, since the mask had no use in life, it was worn only by the actor.

When one speaks of the history of drama, it is important, perhaps more important than anything else, to ask: *Where is the mask?* In the audience, or on the stage? In the theater, or in life? It is here *or* there, never both at once. The most brilliant periods of drama, those in which the mask is triumphant on the stage, are those in which hypocrisy ceases to mask life. On the contrary, those in which what Condorcet calls "the hypocrisy of manners" is triumphant are the very periods in which the mask is snatched from the face of the actor and he is required to be not beautiful but natural; that is to say, if I rightly understand, that he must take his models from reality, or at least from the semblances of it to be seen in his audience; and that is to say, from a monotonous and already masked humanity. The author, meanwhile, also priding himself on being natural, will undertake to furnish the actor a drama suited to his purposes: a drama both monotonous and masked—in short, a drama in which the tragedy of situations (since we must have tragedy of some sort) will gradually replace the tragedy of character. Just consider, for example, the disquieting dearth of characters in the naturalistic novel, the very one that pretends to copy reality. But is this surprising? Our modern society with its Christian morality does all it can to hamper the development of character. "Ancient religion," wrote Machiavelli long ago, "beatified only men of worldly glory like captains of armies and founders of republics, whereas our own has glorified humble and contemplative men rather than men of action. It has found the sovereign good in humility, in abjection, in contempt of worldly things, whereas the other found it in greatness of soul, in strength of body, in all that makes men bold. Our religion wants men strong to endure, not to do great deeds." With characters like these, if we can still call them characters, what kind of dramatic *action* is still possible? Whoever says drama says character; Christianity

269

tions of wealth, unforeseen contributions from the outside account for much in the formation of character;
nevertheless I believe we are led to overestimate the
formative role of such things; I rather believe their role
is one of discovery, merely. All things have always existed
in man, sometimes seen, more or less, and sometimes
hidden; what in recent times has been discovered in him
is newly disclosed to sight but had been there asleep in
man from the beginning. Just as I believe there still exist
in our time people like the Princesse de Clèves, or
Onuphre, or Celadon, I am also quite ready to believe
that long before they appeared in books, Adolphe, Ras-
tignac, and even Julien Sorel existed in life. Furthermore,
I believe that just as humanity is after all stronger than any
particular race, we can find elsewhere than in St. Peters-
burg (I mean in Brussels or in Paris) such characters as
Nezhdanov, Myshkin, and Prince André. But as long as
their voices have not sounded in books or on the stage, they
languish or fret under the mantle of custom, awaiting
their hour. We do not hear them because the world hears
only those voices it can recognize; and because their
voices are drowned out, being too new. We look at the
black mantle of custom and do not see them under it;
better still (I mean worse still), these new forms of
humanity do not recognize themselves. How many secret
Werthers were unaware of themselves, waiting only for
the bullet of Goethe's Werther, to kill themselves! How
many hidden heroes there are, only awaiting the example

of the hero of some book, a spark of his life to make them live, a word of his to make them speak! Is that not, ladies and gentlemen, what we likewise hope from the theater: that it offer humanity new forms of heroism and new heroes?

The soul requires heroism; but our society scarcely allows today more than a single form of heroism (if it is heroism), and that is the heroism of resignation, of acceptance. When a powerful creator of characters, like Ibsen, drapes the figures of his theater in the dreary mantle of our manners, at the same stroke he condemns his most heroic heroes to bankruptcy. Yes, his admirable theater, necessarily, shows us from one end to the other the bankruptcy of heroism. How could he have done otherwise without deserting reality, since, for that matter, if reality allowed any heroism (I mean apparent or theatrical heroism) we should know it, we should indeed know these real heroes personally.

That is why I believe the bold task of Pygmalion or Prometheus is only for those who will deliberately turn the orchestra pit into a moat, widen the gap between stage and audience, between fiction and reality, between actor and spectator, and between the hero and the mantle of manners.

That is why my eyes, full of expectation and joy, are turned toward those unplayed plays of which I spoke awhile ago; they are becoming year by year more numerous and soon I hope will find their stage. Every turn of the wheel of history brings to light what before was invisible in the darkness.

"Time in its slow, illimitable course," says the Ajax of Sophocles, "brings all to light and buries all again; strange things it brings to pass. . . ." We expect of humanity new manifestations. Sometimes those who take the floor keep it for a terribly long time; generations that have yet to speak, however, are growing impatient in their silence. It seems that those who are now speaking, despite their pretense to represent all mankind in our time, must realize that others are waiting, and when these take the floor, those will not get it again—for a long time. The floor today belongs to all who have not yet spoken. Who are they?

The theater will tell us.

I am reminded of the "deep sea" of which Nietzsche speaks, of those unexplored regions of man, full of new dangers and surprises for the heroic navigator. I am reminded of what voyages must have been before there were maps and without our exact and limited record of the known. And I reread the words of Sinbad: "And, lo, the master of the ship vociferated and called out, threw down his turban, slapped his face, plucked his beard, and fell down in the hold of the ship by reason of the violence of his grief and rage. So all the merchants and other passengers came together to him and said to him: 'O master, what is the matter?' And he answered them:

'Know, O company, that we have wandered from our course, having passed forth from the sea in which we were, and entered a sea of which we know not the routes." I am thinking of Sinbad's ship, and how today the theater is turning its back on reality and lifting anchor.

A NOTE ON THE TYPE

The text of this book is set in Caledonia, a Linotype face designed by W. A. Dwiggins. Caledonia belongs to the family of printing types called "modern face" by printers—a term used to mark the change in style of type-letters that occurred about 1800. Caledonia borders on the general design of Scotch Modern, but is more freely drawn than that letter.

The book was composed, printed, and bound by Kingsport Press, Inc., Kingsport, Tennessee.